D1530264

Value Rx

FOR HEALTHCARE

Value Rx

FOR HEALTHCARE

How to Make the Most of
Your Organization's Assets and Relationships

Edward J. Giniat and Barry D. Libert

HarperBusiness

An Imprint of HarperCollins*Publishers*

Book design by Ken Silvia Design, illustration of figures and page layout by Bruce Sanders Design & Illustration.

Library of Congress Cataloging-in-Publication Data has been applied for.

ISBN 0-06662095-3

To Margaret, Andrew, and Matthew, with my love.
You are my true source of happiness.
— EG

To Ellen, Michael, and Adam, for giving me the strength to
help align what we all value in our lives — relationships — with what business
needs to value and measure every day.
— BL

THE VALUE TEAM

CONTRIBUTORS
Alan J. Gayer, Tony Grimsditch,
George Norsig, Andrew North, Steve Orr,
John F. Tiscornia, and Brian D. Wong.

ADVISORS
Kirk McInerney, Helen Rees, and Les Tuerk.

EDITORS
Donna Carpenter, Maurice Coyle,
Deborah Horvitz, Toni Porcelli, Cindy Sammons,
Robert W. Stock, and Ellen K. Wolfe.

REVIEWERS
Jeannot Blanchet, James W. DeLoach, Bill Dwyer,
Robert Hodgkinson, Alister L. Hunt, Greg Jonas,
and Sridhar Ramamoorti.

MARKETERS
Robert Brooks, Barbara Casey,
Celia Ellingson, Mark Fortier,
Lynn Goldberg, Mike Hatcliffe,
Barbara Cave Henricks, Luis Hernandez,
Joe Magliochetti, Eileen Rochford,
Michael Shmarak, and Richard Terrell.

DESIGNERS
Robin Cheung, Max Harless, Kathy Murray,
Bruce Sanders, and Ken Silvia.

PROJECT ADMINISTRATORS
Trish Callahan, Nancy Cutter, Susan Higgins,
Maryellen Mascitti, Debra E. Moderow,
Barbara Nelson, and Jean-Eric Penicaud.

CONTENTS

PART 1 **WHAT MATTERS NOW?**
ASSETS AND RELATIONSHIPS

1 THE SECRET OF SUCCESS TODAY. **7**
2 DO YOU MEASURE WHAT YOU VALUE? **23**
3 IT IS TIME TO MANAGE WHAT YOU VALUE. **39**

PART 2 **WHO'S MANAGING THE ASSETS AND**
RELATIONSHIPS THAT MATTER NOW?

4 WHO'S CREATING VALUE WITH PHYSICAL ASSETS? **55**
5 WHO'S CREATING VALUE WITH FINANCIAL ASSETS? **71**
6 WHO'S CREATING VALUE WITH EMPLOYEES AND SUPPLIERS? **83**
7 WHO'S CREATING VALUE WITH CUSTOMERS? **99**
8 WHO'S CREATING VALUE WITH ORGANIZATION ASSETS? **117**

PART 3 **HOW CAN YOU MANAGE THE ASSETS AND**
RELATIONSHIPS THAT MATTER NOW?

9 SEE AND BUILD YOU BUSINESS MODEL. **145**
10 TAKE AND MANAGE RISK LIKE AN ASTUTE INVESTOR. **163**
11 CONNECT THE SOURCES OF VALUE YOU OWN WITH THOSE YOU DON'T. **183**
12 MEASURE AND MANAGE ALL YOUR SOURCES OF VALUE. **201**
13 IT'S TIME TO MANAGE WHAT MATTERS IN HEALTHCARE. **215**

SOURCES **231**
INDEX **239**

WHAT MATTERS NOW?

ASSETS AND RELATIONSHIPS.

Scientists in the 1950s discovered

that each DNA molecule is composed of two long

strands that take the form of a double helix.

The strands are complementary, each containing

information necessary to reconstruct the other.

By a process of separation and replication,

identical chromosomes are produced for cell after cell,

all of which can be traced to the single original cell that

was formed when sperm and egg united. Taken together,

these chromosomes make up the human genome.

But a malign force, such as radiation,

can damage DNA by upsetting the proper sequence

of its transmission, causing genetic mutations that are

passed on to the next generation.

Assets and Relationships, we argue,

are the economic DNA of the business genome.

Like their living counterparts, an organization's

assets and relationships combine, recombine,

and interact in infinite ways to create economic value.

In other words, organizations create unique expressions

of themselves using different combinations

of the same assets and relationships.

For healthcare companies in particular,

and enterprises in general, the chief goal is

to create value, rather than destroy it.

In today's economy, that means learning

how to build and acquire a well-balanced

portfolio of assets and relationships.

It's time to manage what matters!

1 THE SECRET OF SUCCESS TODAY.

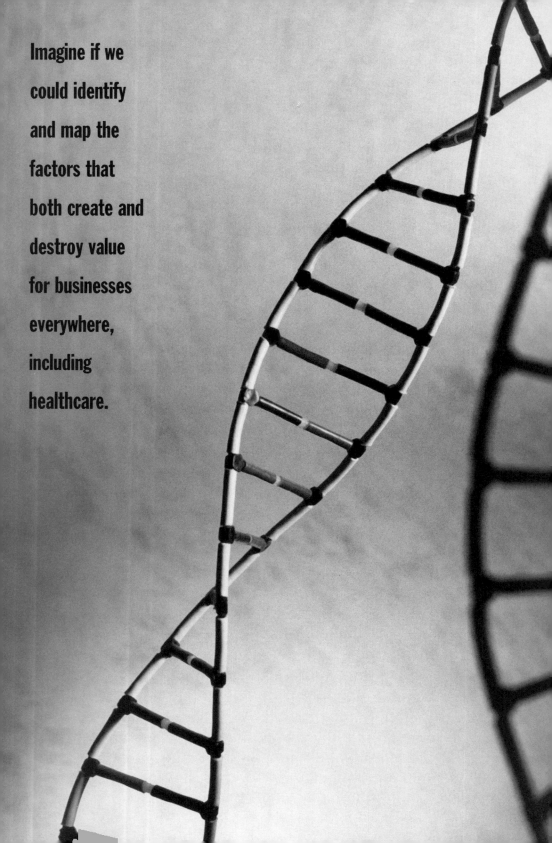

Imagine if we could identify and map the factors that both create and destroy value for businesses everywhere, including healthcare.

"We've discovered the secret of life."
— Francis Crick, *February 1953.*

Gregor Mendel, an Austrian monk born in 1822, had a talent for math and a passion for horticulture.

By pursuing those interests further than others had dreamed, Mendel laid the foundations for genetics, which is to say, the fascinating and profoundly important science of how life continuously evolves.

As a monk at the Brno monastery in what is now Moravia, Mendel conducted a series of plant-breeding experiments, crossing multiple generations of peas to test for resultant characteristics, such as height, color, and shape. Eventually, he recorded the breeding characteristics of some 30,000 plants in the monastery gardens. From these, he formulated mathematical ratios describing the probability of transmission of hereditary characteristics from one generation of peas to the next.

For nearly 50 years, Mendel's published deductions were largely ignored, gathering dust on library shelves. But buried in his records was a hypothesis that would eventually describe and explain our molecular heritage. He suggested that certain hereditary factors — some recessive, others dominant — governed the characteristics of offspring and their abilities to survive and thrive. Those factors are what we now call genes, the basic DNA units that carry the hereditary information of every living organism. Yet, the scientific luminaries of the day, including Charles Darwin, overlooked, or even denied, the significance of Mendel's work.

Mendel died in 1884, two decades before his research was recognized as a breakthrough. Eventually scientists began to focus on the gene's role and its role in passing characteristics from generation to generation. In the early 1950s, two former physicists, James Watson, an American, and Francis Crick, an Englishman, working with viruses and *E. coli* bacteria in petri dishes, discovered how genetic characteristics are passed from one generation to the next. The secret lay in the double-helix structure of a single molecule of deoxyribonucleic acid, otherwise known as DNA.

The double helix contains four chemical bases — adenine, cytosine, guanine, and thymine, which are represented by the letters A, C, G, and T. These chemicals endlessly combine and recombine, producing the astonishing multiplicity of life on earth. That stunning discovery, for which Watson and Crick received Nobel Prizes in 1962, stands as possibly the greatest scientific discovery of all time.

Still, it was not until June of 2000 that scientists succeeded in identifying the billions of chemical combinations that make up the human genome. This first rough map of the genome offers an internal landscape of almost unimaginable complexity. Matt Ridley, former science editor of *The Economist*, offers this vivid perspective:

> If I read the genome out to you at a rate of one word per second for eight hours a day, it would take me a century.
> If I wrote out the human genome, one letter per millimeter, my text would be as long as the River Danube. This is a gigantic document, an immense book, a recipe of extravagant length, and it all fits inside the microscopic nucleus of a tiny cell that fits easily upon the head of a pin.

Ridley believes that "being able to read the human genome will tell us more about our origins, our evolution, our nature, and our minds than all the efforts of science to date. It will revolutionize anthropology, psychology, medicine, paleontology, and virtually every other science."

And he isn't alone in his assessment. Writes *Fortune*: "Sequencing the genome is often called 'biology's moon shot.' That's wrong: Getting to the moon was a joy ride to a dead end — it had no lasting effect on our everyday lives. Decoding the genome will trigger developments that will change our daily lives as much as westward expansion changed the U.S."

Can business learn anything from the quest to understand the human genome?

Absolutely.

Consider the concept that, by analogy, every business, like every organism, has a set of gene-like factors — its assets and relationships — that managers can combine and recombine, thus directing a business' growth, profitability, and market value.

Imagine if we could identify and map the factors that both create and destroy value in the healthcare industry — indeed, in every industry. Imagine if we could identify a finite number of fundamental assets and relationships — say, four or five — that in combination form the basis of every business, indeed, of all economic life. Imagine if we could identify those combinations and map the individual and unique business genomes of companies and economies everywhere, helping enterprises make the right investment decisions, and, in the process, mitigate risk and maximize returns.

Many of these combinations of fundamental factors need not be left to the imagination. They already exist. Managers have used them to launch a global revolution in value creation. They have allowed companies of all sizes and types to create unprecedented wealth for all their stakeholders: some $3 trillion of new wealth in just the last 10 years (despite the recent gyrations in the stock markets).

This book asks what are today's most powerful sources of value. It is, as our title suggests, our Rx for creating value in the healthcare industry and in your healthcare organization.

Our investigation of value — how it is created and destroyed — began with the book, *Cracking the Value Code — How Successful Businesses Are Creating Wealth in the New Economy*. In it, we offered a comparison between the natural and business worlds. Just as all life is a function of four chemical bases combining and recombining, we suggested that all organizations can be viewed as functions of their assets and relationships, interacting in infinite combinations.

Then: Tangible assets.
Now: Assets and Relationships.

The previous book asserted that the essence of any business is not its products, markets, or processes, vital as all these may be. Instead, the core of a company, your company — its economic DNA — consists of five sources of value: physical assets, financial assets, organization assets (patents, brands, and the like), and relationships with customers, employees and suppliers.

Our first book had its genesis in a three-year study conducted by our firm, Andersen, in which we researched the financial markets for the performance of 10,000 companies. Since these markets are the final arbiter of a public company's value, we decided to examine them to find out how value is being created in today's economic environment. As the charts on this page and the next indicate, the results were remarkable.

In 1981, as Figure 1.1 shows, the book value and market value of a company were, for all practical purposes, one and the same. In other words, the market was saying that a company's value could be mea-sured by the value of the assets on its bal-ance sheet. These tangi-ble, book-value assets included physical facili-ties and equipment as well as financial capital. By 2000, however, mar-ket value was nearly 4 times book value. Said differently, the portion of value accorded to tangible assets in our

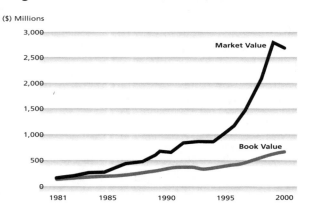

Fig. 1.1 Market Versus Book in All Industries

($) Millions

economy has fallen dramatically. And the new value drivers are intan-gible assets which include intellectual property, knowledge, brands and patents, and relationships. We recognize, too, that assets represented on the balance sheet may have fair values that exceed book value, thus contribute to this widening gap.

What does this mean to your business? Simply that investors have shift-ed their views about what is creating value today. Assets and relationships not found on the balance sheet, such as customers, employees and suppliers, are increasingly being considered sources of the greatest value. Hence, investors are committing larger sums of money and allotting ever-larger premiums to companies that do the same.

As you can see in Figure 1.2, the same trends hold true for the health-care industry. We discovered that this industry had followed a remarkably similar path to success, despite all its statements about "being different." In 1981, the market value of the industry was nearly equal to its tangible assets. But by 2000, the ratio of market value to book value was nearly 9,

Fig. 1.2 Market Versus Book in Healthcare

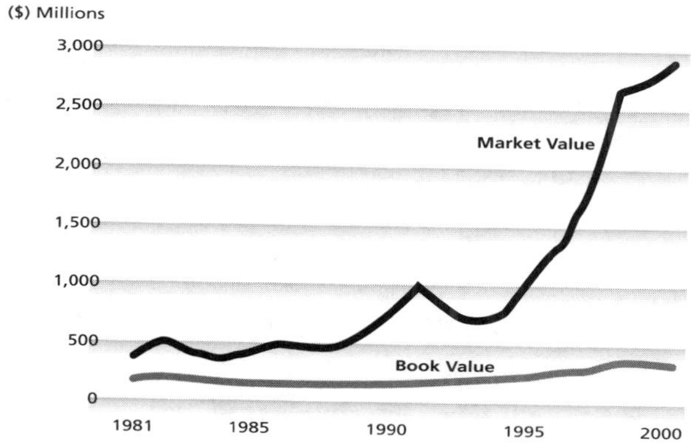

($) Millions

suggesting that those companies in the healthcare industry that invested in intangible assets and relationships were being aptly rewarded.

The message is clear. Investors in healthcare, to an even greater degree than they do in all other industries are, in effect, according less value to brick-and-mortar assets. Moreover, they are increasingly investing in businesses that make the most of their proprietary knowledge, and their relationships with customers, suppliers, and employees.

A Tale of One Industry.

Healthcare stands on the brink of the greatest explosion of new knowledge, new medications, and new technologies in the history of humankind. It also is beset by troubles in virtually every area, buffeted by impatient patients and governments over rising costs and diminished service. As Charles Dickens said of another age, "It was the best of times, it was the worst of times." If healthcare is to take advantage of its unprecedented opportunities in some sectors, and resolve its serious financial and organizational problems in others, it is going to have to learn what creates value across all industries and how to apply that knowledge to itself. In essence, it is time, doctor, to heal thyself.

The industry has never been so big or so essential to the nation's well-

"When a business ceases to add value, it dies, killed by the market, which it has failed to satisfy. That is the principal justification for the market — it roots out the inefficient, and rewards the successful. A successful business is, therefore, **one that continues to add value — forever."**

— Charles Handy.
The Hungry Spirit

being. Healthcare costs Americans more than $1 trillion a year, more than one-sixth of the country's gross domestic product. It includes everything from giant HMOs to solo physicians to not-for-profit teaching hospitals to global pharmaceutical companies. And it touches each one of us personally and directly. We all know that when we or someone we love is physically sick, nothing else matters. We can't concentrate, work, feel enjoyment, participate in, or contribute to, our daily lives.

But much of what we hear about the giant healthcare industry today is disheartening, largely because its business vision is surprisingly small. Some healthcare sectors seem overwhelmed by the same paradox — a constant struggle to perform the duty of care while, at the same time, heeding the necessity to remain financially viable. Others seem to do no wrong as they increasingly participate in our interconnected world economy. The result is a bifurcated industry. Some organizations are frail and faltering, unable to stay abreast of the incredible strides being made in the areas of technology and business-model design. Others are constantly reinventing themselves, prospering right along with the best companies in all other industries.

The result: Although the United States leads the world in scientific advances, and certainly has no dearth of patients (customers by all other accounts), a large portion of the healthcare industry is ailing. For the integrated delivery networks of providers and hospitals (the standard bearers of our care), costs, particularly of prescription drugs, keep increasing, while access to them decreases. HMOs are struggling mightily, physicians' practices are suffering, nursing is on life support, and hospitals that once easily raised capital now find their bonds downgraded because of their poor financial condition. And the entire nursing home industry is in shambles, despite an increase in our elderly population.

Moreover, the number of Americans without health insurance has reached 44 million — more than 1 in 6 people. There is also considerable debate on whether Medicare, which covers millions of older Americans, will pay for prescription drugs.

That view pertains to only one aspect of the industry. The biotechnology sector is once again aglow. Pharmaceutical giants are increasingly gaining strength and worldwide market share. And information services, although struggling today, appear to have an extremely positive outlook as more and more business is done using the newest technologies, including e-commerce software, digital markets, and the Internet. No one can deny the tremendous strength in the medical instruments sector. In short, the healthcare industry is inconsistent in its adaption to a period of remarkable scientific, business, and technological achievement. But the central issue for you is how to use these discoveries to transform your company so that it reaps all the benefits available to it and all those it serves.

The solution depends upon many factors, including your company's ability to identify and efficiently manage the full range of its assets — both tangible and intangible — that constitute its business model and economic DNA.

The potential is awesome for all involved. Consider the discovery we discussed earlier, the decoding of the human genome and the ensuing genetics revolution. It will advance both the early diagnoses of illnesses and the development of drugs to treat them.

A test has already been developed, for example, that spots specific gene mutations that predispose a woman to breast cancer. That knowledge can alert a patient to seek frequent tests, assuring early detection and far better chances of successful treatment than if the cancer is caught in later stages. Other tests are available that can predict heart disease and Alzheimer's disease.

Scientists have created a diagnostic device called a biochip, to which they have attached strands of DNA. These molecular probes, as they are known, can recognize and adhere to their counterparts in a sample of genetic material from a patient. One such test enables scientists to determine which of two types of leukemia a patient has, which makes sure that he or she receives the right treatment. A similar test is being developed that distinguishes among lethal forms of prostate cancer, which often demands intrusive treatment, and less lethal, which may not require any treatment at all.

These developments are, of course, only the beginning of genomic impact on healthcare. Many pharmaceutical companies, for example, are focused on finding products to enhance or prevent the action of particular genes. At least one corporation is studying the proteins produced by the genes that regulate the appetite looking for proteins that can be turned off — a boon for would-be dieters.

Also the hunt is on for so-called therapeutic proteins. One, which enhances skin growth cells, is being tried as a way of treating chronic ulcers. Another therapeutic protein encourages blood-vessel development; researchers hope it can be used to enable the body to bypass the clogged arteries that induce heart disease. Yet another, which has a role in determining the number of blood cells in the body, is under study as a tool for coping with the cell destruction caused by some cancer treatments.

Genetics-based advances are the leading edge of the coming medical revolution. As we will discuss in later chapters, the Internet is already changing the ways in which medical professionals communicate with each other and their patients, as well as the level of medical information available to the latter. The development of greatly improved and minimally invasive surgical equipment has moved into overdrive with the appearance of new electronic devices and more flexible, tougher materials.

Although the United States leads the world in scientific advances, and certainly has no dearth of patients, portions of the healthcare industry get sicker by the month.

Clearly, the future of healthcare is going to be very different from its present — when so many diseases that now require all of a doctor's skill can be diagnosed and treated with gene-based drugs, when hospitals and surgeons experience a gradual lessening in the demand for surgery, when the health insurance business must cope with customers whose medical risks have been much reduced.

The question is, how will your healthcare organization deal with the opportunities and challenges of our economy? Will you recognize the need to rethink your basic attitudes and strategies and redesign your business model to meet those challenges and seize those opportunities? Will you embrace new technologies, take new risks, and measure what really matters, so that your company can align its every activity with what its customers, employees, suppliers, investors, and bondholders want and need according to the research we presented earlier? We hope so. Those questions are at the heart of this book.

The Business of Healthcare Is Business.

Before we go any further, there is one issue that needs repeating: So many of healthcare's leaders and regulators argue vehemently that, because of its mission, healthcare is "different," and does not operate and should not be judged like other industries. But, according to our large-scale research project, just the opposite is true. Healthcare is a business, one that is virtually identical to others in the ways its companies create value — or destroy it. The problem is that many healthcare businesses invest their scarce resources in unproductive assets, then manage those assets so badly they destroy more value than they create.

The most successful enterprises understand that a changing world demands changing responses, including the development of defense and attack strategies when invaders approach their gates. The most successful companies also understand that economic success is determined by the assets an organization invests in and the technologies it uses to link them, which is to say, its business model. Business models rule in today's world of value creation. When investors buy stock at certain prices, when agencies rate bonds, or lenders hand over funds, they are judging as to which business models are most likely to create the most value.

For generations, healthcare professionals and managers set themselves apart from other businesspeople by focusing almost exclusively on the humanitarian aspect of their work. Certainly, no one would wish them to lose their commitment to caring. But healthcare managers also need to recognize that the quality of their care and that of the products and services they create are profoundly dependent on the organizations' financial success or failure; and, they need to act upon that recognition. To put it in concrete terms, only a prosperous healthcare company can provide state-of-the-art products and services to its customers.

The oldest healthcare organizations have been the slowest to acknowledge their need to change. Providers have been particularly hard hit. In a 1999 nationwide survey of 129 health systems, 71 percent reported falling margins, 33 percent had to shed at least one physician group, 28 percent dropped a home-health company, and 15 percent divested a hospital.

The flight of capital — investors, customers, employees, or suppliers — from the hospital sector is due, in part, to cutbacks in Medicare. But it also results from the fact that money is being poured into other sectors that are less tangible-asset intensive, particularly the technology sector. In 1999, Moody's, the bond-rating service, downgraded the ratings of 64 hospitals and upgraded only 14. Its competitor, Standard & Poor's, downgraded 62 issues and upgraded only 12. While current conditions have improved, the issue is still the same.

Hoping in vain that physical assets and strong balance sheets would save them, hospitals went on a merge spree in the 1990s, which failed to solve their underlying problems. They also undertook a cost-cutting binge, discarding precious intangible assets, such as nurses and other medical staff. The historically positive relationships between patients and their doctors have been threatened by the financial exigencies of managed care.

And now, healthcare costs are moving up again. Insurer premium increases continued unabated in 2000. Employers are caught in a squeeze: many need to cut benefits, while, at the same time, they are trying to attract and retain employees during the tightest job market in decades.

The Rules of the Rx.

With this book, we seek to help every organization in the healthcare industry create unprecedented value. We have developed four rules that will help you on the journey:

1 See and build your business model.

Healthcare managers, like all managers, need to invest in the most valuable combinations of assets and relationships.

2 Take and manage risk like an astute investor.

"Risk-taking is what leadership is all about," Raymond V. Gilmartin, chairman and chief executive officer of Merck & Company, Inc., likes to say. We agree. Healthcare managers need to take new risks if they want to gain the new rewards associated with today's economy. They need to invest in intangible assets, such as the knowledge and skill of employees or relationships with customers and reconsider traditional brick-and-mortar and financial assets.

3 Connect the sources of value you own with those you don't.

The Internet, wireless communications, and e-commerce are now the technologies that every good manager must embrace to enhance and enable all assets and relationships. Plumbing and electrical systems still work well for brick-and-mortar assets, but information systems and e-commerce are requirements to connect all your assets and relationships.

4 Measure and manage all your assets.

Determine exactly what needs to be measured and reported to ensure that your organization remains on track. Abandon the idea that intangible assets and relationships are neither measurable nor manageable. It is time to measure and manage all your sources of value, despite how they are labeled, to everyone who matters both inside and outside your organization.

Who will benefit? Anyone and everyone who is part of or touched by the industry: institutional and retail investors; healthcare managers, employees, and professionals; academics, regulators, and corporate buyers of health plans; individual customers, doctors, taxpayers; and, last but not least, patients.

We wish to address these constituencies from the widest possible perspective. We are including in our definition of healthcare the following sectors: hospitals, nursing homes, health systems, medical products, distributors, medical practitioners, insurers, HMOs, e-business, pharmacies, pharmaceutical, biotechnology, information technology, and genomics companies.

▶ What's Next?

 This book offers a core prescription: All healthcare organizations — ranging from not-for-profit hospitals to biotechnology concerns — survive and thrive depending on the assets and relationships in which they invest in order to build their business models. Just as gene alterations in human physiology can lead to disease, ill-considered relationships and asset combinations can lead to unhealthy business models. By the same token, savvy asset combinations can lead to powerful, value-creating business models.

Here's What Lies Ahead.

Part 1 — What Matters Now?

This section of the book explains what created value in the past and what creates value now. We apply our experience and research in financial markets (both the stock and bond markets) to an analysis of the problems and promise of the entire healthcare industry. Identifying the factors that are involved in value creation across all industries, we focus on the various healthcare sectors to glean insight into patterns of value creation and destruction.

Part 2 — Who's Managing The Assets And Relationships That Matter Now?

In this section, which is based on case studies and best-practices, we show who is creating value and how they are going about it. Our hope is that these examples will inspire you to look anew at your organization's business genome and ask: What can we do differently? What new assets and relationships do we need to invest in and manage? What technologies are essential to our success?

Part 3 — How Can You Manage The Assets And Relationships That Matter Now?

In the final section, we offer a guide to how your organization can become a value creator. That guide is predicated on the assumptions of our thesis: If you can truly understand your company's economic DNA, its business genome, then you can find new ways to view, invest in, and manage its assets and relationships to create value. Here, we detail, with rich examples, the four rules introduced in this chapter that will enable you to transform your organization's value power.

Who will inspire your organization to action? You. If you wait for others to step forward, your company's window of opportunity will certainly close.

The journey begins in the next chapter, in which we explain and expand upon the Value Rx.

2 DO YOU MEASURE WHAT YOU VALUE?

Healthcare leaders have failed to resolve the limitations of traditional measurement systems. They must recognize the fact that tangible assets and relationships are losing value, while intangibles are crucial to creating it.

"Everyone measures according to his own shoes."
— *German proverb.*

Accurate measurement is essential to human thinking, creating, navigating, and caring. You can't make decisions, connections, money, or music without true measurements.

You can't run a business or cure a disease without good numbers any more than you can play tennis without a net. A measured life is usually well spent; an unmeasured life is often misspent.

Measurement is, quite simply, the process of quantifying capacities, dimensions, distances, length of time, and so forth by identifying what is considered good and bad, high and low, successful and unsuccessful. For example, an altimeter expresses in feet how high you are; a thermometer tells you in degrees whether it is warm or cold; a yardstick, also in feet, shows you if something is long or short; and a scale informs you in pounds whether it is time to diet or not.

Without the capacity to measure, we would be uncertain, literally, as to where we stand and where we are going. We would not know if we are rich or poor, hot or cold, old or young. The very word "measure"

"Today's Economy makes human capital the most important asset, they can't afford the fixed costs of large payrolls in turbulent times.

pervades all fields, from carpentry to playing music, tailoring to opinion polling. It even has moral overtones, as when we "take a man's measure" or decide whether someone has "measured up."

Measurement shapes how we think of ourselves and the world around us. It establishes what we value and what we shun. And it provides a roadmap, if we know how to read it, that informs our decisions about where we should invest our precious savings and where we should not.

In business, what companies and their leaders measure and manage reveals who they are, what they value, and what assets and relationships they invest in. Performance measures, for example, alter people's behavior and implicitly reflect a company's perception of value. To the degree that your company fails to measure a source of value for all that it is worth, it hobbles its performance, since companies can't effectively manage what they don't measure. And when you label some sources of value such as people as expenses, you view them as expendable.

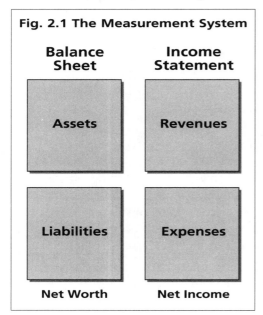

Fig. 2.1 The Measurement System

Balance Sheet	Income Statement
Assets	Revenues
Liabilities	Expenses
Net Worth	Net Income

In traditional measurement systems, income statements determine how well we are doing (revenues, for example) and where we are spending our time and energy (expenses, such as employee wages, for example). Balance sheets show what has enduring value (inventory and real estate), and what reduces that value (debt and accounts payable).

yet, paradoxically, companies are finding

—Robert Reich, former U.S. Labor Secretary.

The net worth, or book value, of an organization is defined by subtracting total liabilities from the total assets on the balance sheet (see Figure 2.1). As a result, traditional measurement systems treat the assets that define book value — which is to say, tangible assets — as the only ones that contribute to the actual worth of a business. But is that right in an era propelled by people and ideas, where innovation and creativity truly count, and where research and development in the healthcare industry have allowed us to map the human genome? Do our current measurement and management systems reflect these expenditures as sources of value? Sadly, no.

Today's measurement system sufficed during the Industrial Age, when a company's profits depended upon its capacity to wring the maximum benefit from its financial and physical assets in order to produce and market a tangible product as inexpensively as possible. Managing this process required measuring the interactions of people within their physical environments. But, as we noted above, the Information Age requires a different focus, in our daily business activities, one in which new sources of value reign supreme. Today's economy is increasingly being driven not through brick and mortar or raw materials, but through the value of intangibles, such as patents, unique processes, and other types of proprietary knowledge as well as relationships with customers, employees, suppliers, and investors. Yet, our existing measurement and management systems still fail to give these value-creating assets their full due.

Who: Medtronic, Inc.
How: It knows the value of its proprietary knowledge.

Medtronic, Inc., a $5-billion manufacturer of medical devices, has recognized the interdependence of its assets and relationships. Medtronic's business is selling ideas and its business model centers on many intangible assets. By making the most of its financial assets, it has greatly increased the performance of its proprietary-knowledge assets and has created new value for shareholders, as well.

Here's how: In 1991, shortly after William W. George became its chief executive officer, Medtronic, then a pacemaker manufacturer, reached a settlement in a number of patent-infringement suits. Opting to take the payments in the form of royalties that continue into the twenty-first century, George used the money to fund research and development. Doing so has catapulted the Minneapolis, Minnesota-based company into a dominant position as a diversified manufacturer of medical devices.

Medtronic increased spending on R&D from between 8 and 9 percent of revenues to 11 percent. At the former rate, according to George, resources were barely meeting the needs of the core business. The increased investment has funded about a dozen new ventures.

George made a list of medical problems and illnesses in need of attention and challenged the Medtronic teams to capitalize on their strengths and address these areas. The impressive results include devices and ther-

"The biggest financial question of our time: When as much as 90 percent of the market value of companies today is not represented on the balance sheet, how do we determine the worth of those intangible assets?" — Michael S. Malone, *editor, Forbes ASAP.*

apies aimed at treating a host of serious medical conditions, such as Alzheimer's disease, cerebral palsy, congestive heart failure, and amyotrophic lateral sclerosis (also known as Lou Gehrig's disease).

Potentially, these breakthroughs could translate into billions of dollars in revenues for Medtronic and incalculable improvements in the collective quality of life for those suffering from excruciatingly painful syndromes.

Many executives would have used the 1991 cash windfall as a one-time boost to net income. George saw it as an opportunity to establish or develop the intellectual underpinnings of his company and thereby increase its value.

In most companies today, intangible assets and relationships are not recognized or counted when determining a company's worth. Pharmaceutical companies, for example, tend to measure the size of and investment in their manufacturing and distribution facilities, but not the information that flows through those buildings, the intellectual capital represented by the employees and researchers who work there.

Healthcare and All Leaders Should Know Better.

As we discussed in Chapter 1, Andersen conducted an in-depth quantitative study of 10,000 companies and their stock-market performances acrosss all industries.

The research pointed to a significant problem not just for healthcare businesses in today's economic environment, but for all companies: the remarkable transformation in terms of what is creating unprecedented wealth is occurring within all industries. We wanted to know if business leaders were keeping pace by installing management and measurement systems that allowed them to make informed decisions about the intangible assets and relationships that the markets rewarded.

So, in 1998, Andersen sponsored another research project, conducted by DYG, Inc., a leader in the field of social and market research. This project was qualitative in nature, and examined how top executives in major U.S. companies in all industries view business success from the perspective of what they managed and measured. Telephone interviews were conducted with more than 700 executives, 20 percent of whom worked in healthcare.

The healthcare sample included leaders of hospitals, health systems, HMOs, health plans, insurers, and biotechnology, pharmaceutical, medical-equipment, and supply companies. And they were asked to restrict their answers to the near future, specifically the next three to five years.

Without measurement, we would be uncertain, literally, as to where we stand and where we are going.

In dramatic fashion, the study, which was conducted twice — first in the spring of 1998 and again in the fall of 2000 — showed a major discrepancy between what leaders said was valuable and what, in fact, they measured. To be specific, the research revealed the following:

1 Healthcare executives emphasize customer relationships and hiring and retaining the right employees as the top two elements of business success. However, for healthcare leaders, innovation rounds out the top three priorities and is emphasized by these executives more than by their colleagues in other industries.

2 Although healthcare executives say maximizing customer relationships and hiring and retaining the right employees are two crucial aspects of business success, they report that the strategies their companies need to pursue these goals are not yet in place. There is a clear lack of alignment between goals and practices on these key issues. In this area, little, if any, progress has been made in the past two years.

3 Healthcare executives acknowledge that a great deal of measurement is taking place at their companies. However, not all areas receive the same level of measurement.

Employee turnover is measured by only 81 percent of our respondents' organizations. That means nearly 20 percent of the healthcare executives do not measure this key indicator.

Customer turnover is measured at just 61 percent of the survey participants' companies. So almost 40 percent don't count the loss of another key source of value.

And the negative statistics continue: Just 54 percent of our respondents measure market share, 40 percent measure brand-image awareness, 39 percent measure the return on research-and-development investments, 39 percent measure the cost of acquiring customers, and a scant 36 percent measure supplier turnover.

"The bottom line is where it belongs — **at the bottom.**"

4 When asked what is very important for their companies to measure over the next few years, the respondents listed, unsurprisingly, customers and employees first. Yet, there is considerable discrepancy between the percentage of respondents who say that these factors are, in general, critical to success and the percentage who actually measure them. Moreover, respondents disagreed as to the specific measures to employ.

> "There will be nothing . . . except e-companies. That does not mean that brick-and-mortar will go away, but click-and-mortar will become the only means of survival."
>
> — John T. Chambers, *chief executive officer, Cisco Systems, Inc.*

What the survey demonstrates so clearly is that healthcare executives recognize what creates value today — customer relationships, employee relationships, and knowledge — but in most cases are failing to manage their enterprises in accordance with their insights. Healthcare leaders are surrounded by companies that are managing hitherto unrecognized assets, such as people and processes, but, thus far, have done little to follow suit. The implications are startling for your company and the healthcare industry:

1 Healthcare executives' definition, and order of priority, of near-term, critical-success factors is consistent with the findings of our 10,000-company research project. The notable exception is the low priority that healthcare executives accord to supplier relationships. This is problematic, given its high use of suppliers of services, such as doctors and nurses.

— Paul Hawken, *founder, chairman, and chief executive officer, Smith & Hawken, Inc.*

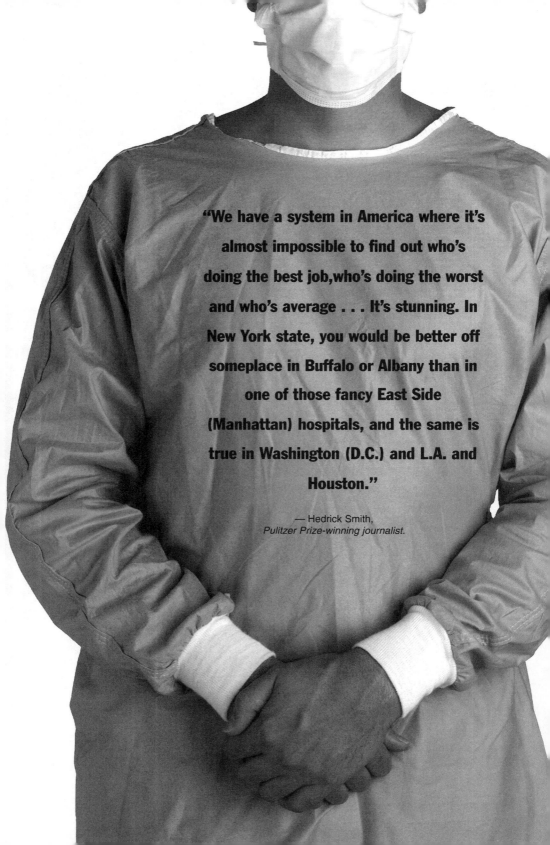

"We have a system in America where it's almost impossible to find out who's doing the best job, who's doing the worst and who's average . . . It's stunning. In New York state, you would be better off someplace in Buffalo or Albany than in one of those fancy East Side (Manhattan) hospitals, and the same is true in Washington (D.C.) and L.A. and Houston."

— Hedrick Smith,
Pulitzer Prize-winning journalist.

2 Current initiatives to measure and manage these sources of value are often not seen as necessary for success. The executives in our survey admit that they should be putting these initiatives above all else.

3 The fact that measurement systems are not currently in place for even the most critical sources of value implies that executives in the healthcare industry may not be fully in control of their management systems — a frightening thought given that their mission is to provide care.

4 The lack of future measurement indicates that the industry's problems could continue for some time. In any case, our question to you is, do you measure what you value and, if not, are you establishing the necessary processes and systems to inform your decisions and fuel your success in this arena? In either case, *take the test at the end of the chapter to see if your company measures what it values.*

The healthcare industry is not alone in its failure to measure, let alone truly manage, what is valuable. The misconceptions and miscalculations about sources of value have effects on the macro-economic front as well. Consider the United States' trade deficit, now the largest of all time. Let's suppose that in a given quarter, U.S. consumers buy 1,000 cars made in Japan at an average price of $10,000. At the same time, MSN, the creation of Microsoft Corporation, offers Japanese visitors to its various Web sites entertainment, the ability to purchase tickets, access to investment information, and the capacity to visit the world — virtually that is.

All the government's economists, including the U.S. Federal Reserve chief, Alan Greenspan, would look at those two groups of transactions and simply add $10 million to our trade deficit. That is because, by all traditional measures, MSN is creating no stateside value to match the car sales, despite the fact that it has many users, some of whom make purchases.

The Federal Reserve notwithstanding, there's something missing from the equation. MSN has developed a huge, loyal customer base, which now numbers in excess of 200 million. MSN's customer base is not an abstract concept; it is extremely valuable and value-producing, and the trade deficit should reflect that fact.

A notable example of the failure to measure the value of intangible sources of value on a major scale was the national balance sheet prepared by the Japanese government in October 2000. It was very strong in terms of the nation's liabilities, including the trillions of dollars that will be paid to pensioners. Yet, on the other side of the ledger, more than 40 percent of the government's assets were in the form of loans to local governments and public corporations, many of which are close to bankruptcy.

If you looked only at the balance sheet, you might conclude that Japan was about to go under. Constricted by conventional measures, the government was forced to scratch for extra assets. Among them were trees that the government owns in forests and fields, as well as individual trees near buildings — 6.7 million of the latter. The value put on each tree: $150.

Yet, how short-sighted and unrealistic is such a measure of that nation's worth. It omits its most important sources of value: the creativity and energy of its people — and there are 125 million of them. Could it be that all these people know nothing, create nothing, and know no one?

Is Japan bankrupt? Hardly. If the value of its people was factored into the equation, its abundance would be obvious. But the leaders of Japan, like executives from healthcare and other industries we polled, were not measuring what they truly valued.

Given the importance of this issue, what can and should be done in your company as well in society at large?

"If we're spending considerably more than a trillion dollars — more than any other country by far — on a system that's dysfunctional, then we're wasting 15 percent of our GNP. . . . We're making a bad buy, not just in economical terms, but safety terms. We do worse, and we spend more getting there. And that's just silly."— Arthur Levin, *consumer-health advocate.*

The first step is to increase your understanding of what actually creates value so that you can begin to measure the entirety of your healthcare company's assets. The second step is to find new ways to measure the value of all sources of value, with a special concern for employee and customer relationships, as well as other difficult-to-measure intangibles. And the third step is to join in the discussion that is currently being waged on exactly this issue.

The ability to see, invest in, manage, and measure intangible assets and relationships, we believe, is key to success today. And that is true for every kind of company in every kind of industry and for every kind of stake-holder — investors, bondholders, customers, employees, or suppliers. Healthcare must alter its approach to the assets and relationships its exec-utives say are most valuable and the assets and relationships they actually measure. Of course, too much is at stake for wholesale changes in the mea-surement system to be made overnight — but the dialogue has begun. And the time to confront these realities is now.

▶ What's Next?

To survive and thrive, the healthcare industry must confront the *zeitgeist*, the outlook and spirit, of its current measure-ment models, which take a fundamental stand on what has value. Do healthcare leaders have the skills and the will to allocate their resources more efficiently on behalf of their organizations' and industry's crucial economic mission?

Chapter 3 offers insight into the process of building business models that create value, and it introduces the Value Dynamics Framework. With it, we turn these nagging questions into plausible, practical answers for healthcare managers, and we do so in language that every-one can see, understand, and use in his or her daily business activities.

In the first exercise, we offer a tool for assessing what factors you believe to be most critical to your company's success. Your answers to the questions raised in the second exercise will help you determine how closely your practices match those priorities.

Exercise 1

Rate the following items. Are they important to your success in the next three to five years?	Not Important	Somewhat Important	Very Important
1. Keeping sufficient cash on hand.	❏	❏	❏
2. Raising equity and debt capital.	❏	❏	❏
3. Increasing revenues and earnings.	❏	❏	❏
4. Maintaining efficient facilities.	❏	❏	❏
5. Operating effective equipment.	❏	❏	❏
6. Optimizing inventories.	❏	❏	❏
7. Establishing and maintaining positive relationships with customers.	❏	❏	❏
8. Developing strong channels of distribution.	❏	❏	❏
9. Fostering positive community relations.	❏	❏	❏
10. Hiring and retaining the right employees.	❏	❏	❏
11. Motivating employees.	❏	❏	❏
12. Establishing and maintaining positive relationships with suppliers.	❏	❏	❏
13. Creating new products and services.	❏	❏	❏
14. Developing culture and values.	❏	❏	❏
15. Building optimal systems and processes.	❏	❏	❏
16. Developing and maintaining strong brands.	❏	❏	❏
17. Implementing e-commerce capabilities.	❏	❏	❏

Here are some suggestions for analyzing the results:

If, in Exercise 1, you indicated that you considered the first six items to be very important to your company's success, you are very much in the mainstream of healthcare companies. These items are all concerned with tangible assets, both physical and financial. If, however, you also rated the remaining items in Exercise 1 as very important, you are ahead of the pack. These items are all concerned with intangible assets like customer and employee relationships. Items 7 thru 17 reflect the assets that are of greatest sources of value in today's economy.

Now, look once more at your responses to the first six items in Exercise 1, and see how they match up with your responses to the first six items in the Exercise 2. We suspect you will find that they correspond very well — in other words, you measure the physical and financial assets that you hold to be most critical to success.

But when you make that same comparison with the rest of the items in Exercise 1, and the measurements for items 7 through 19 in Exercise 2, you may find a very different story.

Let's suppose, for example, you responded to item 7 in the first exercise by saying that you

Exercise 2

Indicate whether your business currently measures, or plans to measure, the following:

	Currently: Do not measure	Currently: Measure in part	Currently: Measure in full	In the next 3 to 5 years: Will not measure	In the next 3 to 5 years: Will measure in part	In the next 3 to 5 years: Will measure in full
1. Price/earnings ratio.	❑	❑	❑	❑	❑	❑
2. Return on investment.	❑	❑	❑	❑	❑	❑
3. Operating profit.	❑	❑	❑	❑	❑	❑
4. Return on fixed assets.	❑	❑	❑	❑	❑	❑
5. Asset-utilization rate.	❑	❑	❑	❑	❑	❑
6. Inventory turn rate.	❑	❑	❑	❑	❑	❑
7. Customer loyalty.	❑	❑	❑	❑	❑	❑
8. Market share.	❑	❑	❑	❑	❑	❑
9. Cost of customer acquisition and retention.	❑	❑	❑	❑	❑	❑
10. Quality of community relations.	❑	❑	❑	❑	❑	❑
11. Employee turnover.	❑	❑	❑	❑	❑	❑
12. Return on training investment.	❑	❑	❑	❑	❑	❑
13. Supplier turnover.	❑	❑	❑	❑	❑	❑
14. Supply-chain effectiveness.	❑	❑	❑	❑	❑	❑
15. Return on R&D investment.	❑	❑	❑	❑	❑	❑
16. Time to market for new products and services.	❑	❑	❑	❑	❑	❑
17. Lead time to satisfy customer orders.	❑	❑	❑	❑	❑	❑
18. Brand awareness.	❑	❑	❑	❑	❑	❑
19. Percent of revenue from e-commerce.	❑	❑	❑	❑	❑	❑

consider "establishing and maintaining positive relationships with customers" to be highly critical to success. If you then examine your response to item 9 in Exercise 2, you will find out just how much that attitude is reflected in your measurement practices. If you measure the "cost of customer acquisition and retention," you are to be congratulated. In our survey of healthcare executives, only 39 percent said they actually measured that cost.

Or, consider your responses to item 12 in the first exercise and item 13 in the second exercise. If you indicated that "establishing and maintaining positive relationships with suppliers" was "somewhat" or "highly" critical to your company's success, wouldn't it follow that you would go to some pains to make sure that goal is being pursued and the results measured? But do you actually measure those results now? If so, you are an exception. Our survey showed that just 36 percent of respondents kept tabs on supplier turnover.

If the criteria for success that you rated as very important in Exercise 1 are not matched by full current measurement in Exercise 2, then that success is at risk. Further, if that shortfall is not corrected in the next 3 to 5 years, that success, most likely, will not be sustained.

We hope that you use these exercises to gain a clearer sense of your company's attitudes toward both tangible and intangible assets and its relationships. If your company is like most others, you will find a significant discrepancy between your recognition of the importance of some of these intangible assets and your willingness to act upon that conclusion. At a time when the value of companies is increasingly linked to the strength of their intangible assets, like relationships with employees and suppliers, no company can afford such discrepancies.

3
IT IS TIME TO
MANAGE WHAT
YOU VALUE.

Healthcare providers have to make a fundamental shift from seeking market share to gaining customer share, which will require a different response from each healthcare segment.

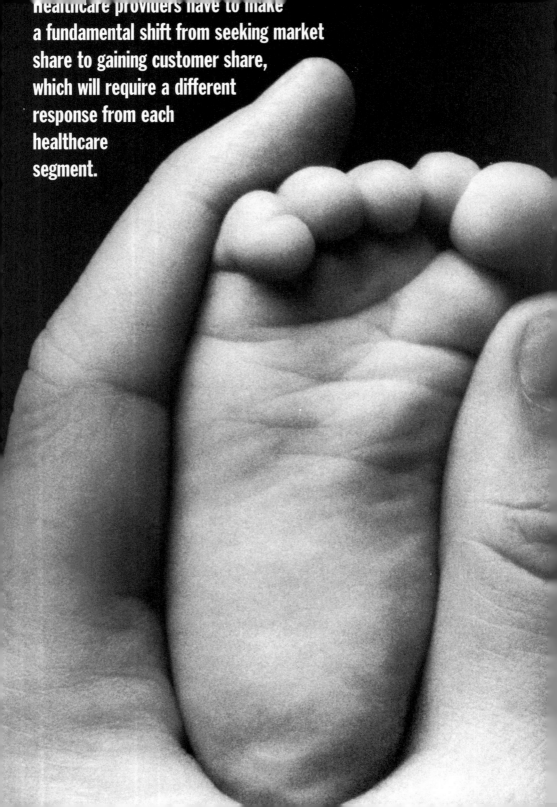

"Don't wait for an SOS to take action."
— Captain D. Michael Abrashoff, *U.S. Navy.*

As the U.S. economy raced into the 1990s, Perkin-Elmer Corporation slowed down.

Once an agile leader in the medical-equipment industry, it was now considered an underperformer, best known for dull instruments and slow growth. Its future was bleak, if not blank — until destiny swooped down in the person of Tony L. White, a visionary with a yen to create second acts for supposed has-beens.

Tony White had spent more than 20 upwardly mobile years at Baxter International, Inc., one of the world's biggest medical-products companies. By most accounts, he had good reason to expect that he would be awarded the top job. When he was passed over, his eye began to wander — in the direction of Perkin-Elmer.

There, White spotted a unique opportunity in the form of a few promising assets the company had recently acquired, but thus far had failed to develop. One was the rights to something called the polymerase chain

> ## "It's easy to decide what you're going to do. The hard thing is deciding what you're not going to do."
>
> — Michael S. Dell,
> *founder, chairman, and chief executive officer, Dell Computer Corporation.*

reaction, or PCR, a chemical process for copying DNA, and the other was Applied Biosystems, Inc., a manufacturer of DNA sequencers that used PCR.

White had a vision of how to turn these two assets into Perkin-Elmer's salvation. The directors of the company were so impressed by his background and his ideas that, in 1995, they named him chief executive officer.

Eventually selling all the assets irrelevant to the business model he envisioned, White renamed the company the PECorporation (today it is called Applera Corporation) and proceeded to redesign its business genome. What emerged was a profoundly new positioning in the marketplace — a holding company comprised of two distinct business units with separate tracking stocks: Applied Biosystems and Celera Genomics Group.

Applied Biosystems, the life-sciences research-system unit, now sells the world's fastest DNA gene sequencers, as well as products for protein research and forensic medicine. Celera Genomics was formed in 1998 to sequence the human genome, the first step in a revolution in both biology and medicine. White scored a coup for Celera when he recruited the founder of the Institute for Genomic Research, a brilliant and controversial geneticist named J. Craig Venter.

At the institute, Venter had been deciphering gene sequences at an unprecedented pace, but White dangled an offer Venter couldn't refuse — the opportunity to build the world's largest gene-sequencing facility. Today, in a textbook case of business synergy, Celera leases 300 high-speed gene-sequencing machines built by its sister company, Applied Biosystems.

In June 2000, White's and Venter's efforts were richly rewarded when Celera announced that it had completed the sequencing of the human genome. That, of course, was only the first chapter of a remarkable story to come. As Venter has noted, "The final chapter will entail a complete understanding of life's processes, such that disease and illness finally can be treated and cured directly at the source."

But let's step back and look at Applera's business genome. After White reinvented the company, adding new assets and creating a different combination of assets and relationships, investors put a much higher value on the company. They recognized that the worth of all its assets and relationships, its business model, could no longer be judged simply on the basis of what was listed on the balance sheet.

Applera's brand, for example, has international recognition as a leader in genetic science. Its customer base, from the largest pharmaceutical companies to the most prestigious academic institutions, is the envy of competitors. Its leadership team has presided over both scientific and business innovations. Yet, none of these crucial, largely intangible assets is included in the traditional measures of business worth.

The Applera story is about business-model redesign — salvaging or discarding undervalued assets and recombining them with others to create a vast amount of previously unrealized value. Its focus on a whole new set of assets and relationships has won over the financial markets and vastly increased its worth.

What worked for Applera, we argue, will work for HMOs, insurers, doctors, and patients, even struggling hospital systems, whose current worth is hostage to the tangible bricks and mortar of its buildings. In this chapter, we offer a tool that we call the Value Dynamics Framework, which will help you see, measure, and manage the assets and relationships that really matter in today's economic environment.

The chief goal of all businesses, including healthcare is to build a business model that creates value, rather than destroys it. In today's economy, that means learning how to build and acquire a balanced portfolio of assets and relationships.

Let's review four guidelines that every healthcare organization must understand in order to manage what matters:

1 Organizations are their assets and relationships, owned and unowned. What distinguishes one organization from another are the ways these assets and relationships are combined and connected to create value.

2 Organizations must understand and take prudent risks as they relate to new combinations of assets and relationships.

3 Organizations must take advantage of today's technology to connect their assets and enrich their relationships

4 Organizations must measure and report their investments in all their assets and relationships.

Who: Albert Einstein Healthcare Network.
How: It redesigned its business model.

A decade ago, the Albert Einstein Healthcare Network fulfilled the intention of a traditional acute-care hospital with hundreds of beds, several operating theaters, and an emergency room. It boasted a first-class reputation and produced sufficient revenue to maintain its operations.

Then, Martin Goldsmith, Einstein's chief executive officer, grew concerned that the hospital was not ready for the massive changes he anticipated for the healthcare industry, including technological breakthroughs, continually rising costs, and an increasing elderly population. Competitors were already setting up outpatient services and disease-prevention programs that tapped new sources of revenue, and Goldsmith feared his institution was falling behind.

His solution was to entirely reinvent his acute-care hospital. He began by redefining Einstein's basic purpose. Instead of seeking to remain a leader among acute-care hospitals, the new Einstein would do whatever was necessary to improve the overall well-being of each individual patient. The new slogan was "We put patients first," and Goldsmith was determined to live up to it.

Encouraging his veteran staff to jettison their comfortable old routines, Goldsmith told them to think of themselves as entrepreneurial risk takers. He built a comprehensive network of health services that included primary care, nursing homes, outpatient services, home care, rehabilitation centers, psychiatric services, and educational programs for patients. With a newly energized staff and an expanded network, Einstein was firmly positioned to recognize and satisfy the present and future needs of its patients. Equally important, it was on track to profit from its overhaul.

What we can learn from Einstein's revamped business model is that major investments in physical assets do not preclude an approach that relies on intangible assets and relationships to create value.

Introducing a New Framework.
Except for Einstein and a handful of other organizations, today's healthcare system is still using an Industrial-Age approach that treats healthcare products and services as though they were widgets. As we

pointed out in our last chapter, the people who provide those products and services are measured as expenses. And consumers are viewed simply as the conduit through which greater revenues are realized.

As our research and everyday experiences make apparent, the old approach is becoming dysfunctional. Assets and relationships long ignored must at the forefront of healthcare practice in today's economy. But, which assets and relationships, and in what proportions? Furthermore, how do they connect and combine to improve economic returns?

Our answer is a new framework, Value Dynamics, that details the entire business genome in today's economy — that is, all the assets and relationships that you can use in your organization to design your business model. We conceived Value Dynamics as a tool for identifying and then unifying all sources of value in today's world using a finite number of elements. We asked ourselves: What are the primary sources of value? Could we classify them in a way that would help businesses understand more clearly how those assets and relationships create and destroy value? If so, businesses could allocate their resources accordingly?

We began with traditional balance-sheet assets — physical and financial assets, two important classes of assets in the business genome. In addition, we needed to identify the other components of the genome, even though traditional measurement systems generally overlook them.

We looked at income statements, which track revenues and expenses. Although they do not directly identify sources of value, income statements can be viewed somewhat like photographic negatives. For example, relationships with buyers of every type are the assets that underlie revenues.

The new Einstein would do whatever was necessary to improve the overall well being of each individual patient. The new slogan was "We put patients first."

Relationships with sellers of every shape — including suppliers, employees, and others who contribute to making products and rendering services — are also assets (even though they appear as expenses on the income statement). In essence, we mined income statements, looking for the true assets and relationships that underlie revenues and expenses. But that was not enough.

The business genome has one more category of assets, which glues the whole together, giving an organization its unique characteristics. We call these assets organization assets and they include such components as systems and processes, culture and values, leadership, and brands.

Then: Two sources of value.
Now: Five sources of value.

These five sources of value — financial, physical, organizational, customer, employee and supplier, — comprise the Value Dynamics Framework. As you can see in Figure 3.1, we have traditional balance-sheet assets on the left side (physical and financial) and our three new sources of value, on the right and in the center. These new sources of value are, in large part, not tracked with performance indicators, even though they are the most important value creators in today's economy.

The Value Dynamics Framework is a tool that helps companies see all their assets and relationships and invest in the ones that matter. It can be used as a high-level strategic template to help you understand how your organization functions in relation to its business genome.

The framework can also be used to develop risk and reward profiles for different assets and relationships, assign management accountability for them, or create new measurements and information flows around them.

The framework suggests a complete view of all the assets and relationships that matter and how they can be combined. Indeed, you can use it to study how your organization creates value *vis a vis* its investments in assets. You can also use the framework to consider significant challenges facing the healthcare industry as a whole. This gives you a very different profile of healthcare's opportunities and challenges, as the following brief analysis suggests.

Physical Assets.
Recorded on the balance sheet, these assets include land, buildings, equipment, and inventory.

Then: Safe.
Now: Risky.

Medical and information technologies are accelerating the rate at which physical assets are becoming obsolete. Healthcare providers need to consider the overcapacity in the market today, which will persist even though our aging population will eventually require more healthcare services. Healthcare providers need to rethink their

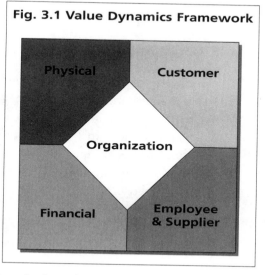

Fig. 3.1 Value Dynamics Framework

Physical

Customer

Organization

Financial

Employee & Supplier

purpose and redesign their facilities and other physical assets — keeping in mind that the delivery of care will become more virtual in the future.

Financial Assets.
These assets are included on the balance sheet. Among them are cash, receivables, investments, debt, and equity.

Then: Result of Value.
Now: Source of Value.

Health systems are torn by daily compromises between long-term needs and short-term demands, with financial assets often the most visible battleground. The capital required for investments that are critical to long-term performance may be competing with cash outlays made to stop the financial bleeding on a daily basis. Healthcare organizations in every sector need to develop strategic options that free capital to create value through appropriate resource allocations, including customer and employee relationships.

Employee and Supplier Relationships.
Not reported on the balance sheet are these relationships with employees and suppliers.

Then: Expenses.
Now: Enduring value.

Today's economy is characterized by a war for talent as industries vie for the best and brightest managers and professionals. Can healthcare compete? Providers are currently experiencing rapid turnover at management and staff levels. In comparison to other industries, compensation is declining. Contentious relationships with physicians, nurses, and other employees are often the cause of value destruction in HMOs and hospitals. For instance, hospitals exacerbated their fiscal problems during the 1990s by acquiring primary-care physician practices, which now have to be divested. Working with physician partners and staff personnel will first require innovative approaches, then new ways to measure value.

Customer Relationships.
These relationships, which aren't on the balance sheet, include connections with customers, distributors and other channels, and affiliates.

Then: Episodic.
Now: Lifelong.

Every healthcare sector is involved when we talk about relationships with customers. Providers have to make a fundamental shift from seeking market share to gaining customer share, which will require a different response from each healthcare segment. Hospitals and health systems, for example, will need to transcend the conventional outlook in medicine — the patient as episodic event — in order to create enduring relationships that will be enacted through both physical and virtual channels.

Organization Assets.

These assets, which are not on the balance sheet, include leadership, strategy, structure, processes, systems, culture and values, brands, and proprietary knowledge.

Then: Unnecessary to quantify.
Now: Vital to quantify.

Healthcare providers often lack clear strategies. Electronic commerce, for example, provides virtually unlimited opportunities for healthcare providers to streamline processes, improve care, and increase patient satisfaction. But the investments are significant and the risks high.

Every organization, of course, uses many different assets and relationships to support a business model. The strength of the Value Dynamics Framework is that it provides a coherent context from which to see, invest in, and manage diverse sources of value.

▶ What's Next?

 Value Dynamics offers a new framework that managers can use to see what matters (all of their sources of value), invest in what matters (the optimal combination of assets and relationships), and manage and measure what matters (versus only physical and financial assets). In the next five chapters, we present a series of case studies to spotlight the sources of value identified in the Value Dynamics Framework, and how enterprises are making the most of them to help create unique business models.

Identifying the assets and relationships that matter is the critical first step toward understanding the business genome — your business model. These best practices are instructive for the entire industry. With our examples as a backdrop, we believe you will perceive your company's business model for what it actually is. Only when you know what your business invests in will you be able to make the right decisions about how to create value.

We begin in Chapter 4 with the most concrete and visible components of value: physical assets.

PART 2

WHO'S MANAGING THE ASSETS AND RELATIONSHIPS THAT MATTER NOW?

When the human body falls ill,

medical science follows a time-honored course

of action: diagnosis, then treatment.

We propose a similar sequence for creating value.

Companies must learn to identify and measure

all their sources of value if they are to

accurately manage what matters.

They must learn to understand themselves as portfolios

of assets and relationships that are endlessly combining

to create economic value. This is the only way to develop

optimum business models and effective treatments.

In the following chapters, we introduce and analyze
the five sources of value
that make up the genome of every organization.
We also show how a wide variety of companies
are making the most of these assets and relationships.

Just as the interaction of four basic chemicals
determines the body's ability to adapt
to the difficulties of our environment, the mix of
assets and relationships within a company will determine its
ability to adapt to the dangers and opportunities
of the economic environment.

Let's take a look at who's managing what matters now.

4 WHO'S CREATING VALUE WITH PHYSICAL ASSETS?

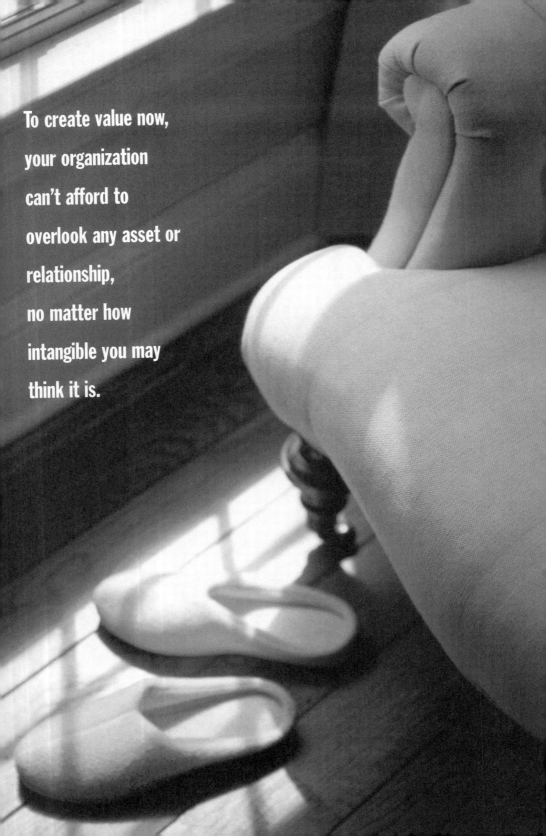

To create value now,
your organization
can't afford to
overlook any asset or
relationship,
no matter how
intangible you may
think it is.

*"Before I built a wall, I'd ask to know
what I was walling in or out."*
— Robert Frost.

What's in a name?
Webster's tells us that the word hospital comes from Latin for "guest room."

The idea of a guest room sounds almost anachronistic if we are using it to describe the huge concrete and steel institutions we call hospitals.

Hospitals are a big business, albeit one struggling to survive under managed care and recent Medicare cutbacks under the U.S. Balanced Budget Act of 1997. In their efforts to alleviate escalating financial problems, hospitals have adopted a variety of strategies, including consolidations, personnel cutbacks, even the elimination of some traditional services. Results have been mixed. New contracts with managed-care companies hold little promise, because most hospitals lack the assets and relationships that would give them negotiating power today.

Acquiring physicians' practices has not brought the desired results; instead of improved revenues from more customer referrals, acquisitions have resulted in an actual decline in doctors' productivity by 15 to 20 percent within 2 years. HMO operations and other non-core businesses have also been financially disastrous. Mergers were not the source of improved revenue or reduced costs that they were hoped to be. Even cost reductions from merged back-office administrative operations have been disappointing.

In 1999, the average hospital in the United States had an operating margin of less than 4 percent. Integrated delivery systems were even worse with operating margins of approximately 2.5 percent. This means a manager's margin for error is extremely small, even before the institution posts a loss.

Pressuring beleaguered hospitals even more, Medicare reductions are expected to force reductions of inpatient margins down to 11 percent in 2001 from a high of 17.1 percent in 1997 — despite the $7 billion in additional spending provided from the relief package that was approved in 1999.

It is necessary that hospitals and other healthcare organizations that invest heavily in physical assets ask: How can we create value now? How can we make the most of all of our assets and relationships? What's the value prescription in today's economy for us and our stakeholders?

From a strictly economic standpoint, one view of what hospitals do is rent space to transient visitors called patients and to the suppliers and distributors (a.k.a. physicians) who treat them. The basic business model for a hospital, then, is centered upon creating value by investing in physical assets — which is to say, land, buildings, and medical equipment.

Hospitals and healthcare organizations, however, must now make the most of not just their physical assets but a host of other sources of value as well. These intangibles include brands, processes, systems, customer relationships, information (that is, business and patient outcomes), even investor knowledge. Managers need to invest in and extract value from tangible and intangible, owned and unowned assets and relationships to create business models that optimize value for their organizations and stakeholders.

"A Scottish friend of mine, the last in a long line
of lairds, was driving an African friend
back from the airport to stay with him
in his castle. As they drove deep
into the highlands, my friend waved his hand
expansively at the heather-covered hills
all around them — 'Now,' he said, 'you are
on my territory, all that you can see belongs
to me.' He wasn't boasting, just explaining, but the
African was puzzled. 'I don't understand,'
he said. 'How can you own a mountain?
That belongs to the earth . . .
Perhaps you mean that you are looking after it
for a while, a sort of trustee, maybe?'
'If you put it like that, yes, I suppose so.'
My friend told me this story a year later.
He said it made him realize
that we let our language shape the way we think.
Of course, he said, ownership was the wrong word."

— Charles Handy,
The Hungry Spirit.

As we have argued in earlier chapters, healthcare leaders in every sector must learn from their own and other industries how to identify the business models that create value today. In order to exploit the full range of their assets and relationships, they need to understand not only which assets to invest in, but in what proportions and combinations.

While many business analysts, ourselves included, are excited about the opportunities that new digital technologies are opening, the key is to remember that all sources of value are essential. Physical assets, such as hardware and medical equipment, are needed for delivering the products and services necessary to treat patients, manage inventory, and house organizations.

Of course, physical assets are measured and accounted for on the balance sheet. Still, their worth can be obscured by traditional measurement systems, because their market value often differs from their book value. Furthermore, the balance sheet fails to indicate whether a particular physical asset is adding to or subtracting from a company's overall value, because the economic environment is always changing.

In today's economy, your healthcare organization can't afford to overlook any source of value, no matter how intangible you may think it is. Leaders must find new ways to create value within all of their assets and relationships, which include, as we will see, their investments in new technologies that are used to enhance physical resources.

In this chapter, we look at a number of healthcare organizations that have excelled at making the most of their physical assets. Our journey takes us into the age-old realm of land and buildings, as well as equipment and inventory. Let's start with land and buildings.

Land and Buildings.

When hunting gave way to farming in early human history, land and the buildings on it became the most precious of all commodities. Not surprisingly, property has always been invested with both commercial and spiritual value. While neighbors built fences to keep people out and livestock in, countries fought bloody wars to maintain their own land or annex someone else's.

In *Travels in France*, Arthur Young wrote: "Give a man the secure possession of a bleak rock, and he will turn it into a garden; give him a nine years' lease of a garden, and he will convert it into a desert." We can apply this notion to the healthcare industry. New hospital construction may appear to be reckless, when facilities around the country are having trouble filling beds. But, on May 1, 1999, Northwestern Memorial Health Care, in Chicago, Illinois opened a $680-million world-class medical complex that looks as though it may very well be a money-making machine rather than a money-leaking spigot.

Who: Northwestern Memorial Health Care. How: It redesigned its properties.

Has the city of Chicago somehow sidestepped the problems plaguing hospitals elsewhere? Are all of its rooms occupied? Hardly. In fact, one in every three beds in greater Chicago remains unused. Nonetheless, Gary Mecklenburg, president and chief executive officer of Northwestern Memorial Health Care, is confident that he can fill all of them. First, the new facility actually contains fewer beds. Encompassing 22 sites and 3 aging inpatient hospitals, the old Northwestern Memorial resulted from a series of mergers and operated with little, if any, integration among the scattered institutions. While the old hospital had 1,093 beds, the new one, reduced to 773, is extensively integrated, and offers an altogether different mix of services.

Taking into account the dramatic changes that managed care and technological innovations have instituted, the designers of the new complex dedicated only 20 percent of the space to beds. The rest is divided into substantial ambulatory care units (the fastest growing area in medical care in the country), diagnostic and therapeutic services, and inviting public areas for visitors. In fact, Mecklenburg worries that there may be too few beds, not too many. He explained:

**In 2000, Northwestern Memorial unveiled
a new strategic plan that included
this overarching goal:
to provide "the best patient experience."
Among its principles for crafting
the best patient experience is a commitment
to creating "a welcoming and supportive environment
for each patient" and to exceeding
patient expectations "from registration
through payment of the bill."**

The beds themselves are apportioned differently than the customary configuration, with a much greater number dedicated to critical and intensive-care patients. The increased demand for outpatient services has changed the emphasis of the inpatient units that now predominantly treat acutely ill patients.

As one might expect, the hospital is awash in other physical assets: high-tech equipment in the clinics, doctors' offices, and operating rooms. For example, the hospital can transmit X-rays digitally between the radiologist's office and the emergency room, which shortens the time that the patient has to wait before a diagnosis or course of treatment can begin.

If doctors welcome innovations such as these for direct patient care, hospital administrators are quick to point out that they reflect the hospital's philosophy of "patients first," adopted in 1987. Proof of the credo is evident in a well-conceived layout that is easy to follow, and an elevator design that eases the flow of traffic. Mecklenburg explained that the new design took shape because managers and architects listened to patients. "We have provided them with an environment . . . they want," he told us, "and that means you are going to achieve higher volume and greater efficiency."

The commitment to "patients first" dictated the facility's twin-tower

design. Designers and administrators reasoned that patients coming to the hospital for outpatient procedures may feel uncomfortable around much sicker individuals who have portable oxygen tanks and IV poles. By the same token, seriously ill patients may want to preserve their privacy and not bump into outpatients as they all move about the hospital. In response, builders planned a 17-story pavilion for inpatients and a 22-story structure reserved for ambulatory care.

Mecklenburg is proud to note that "the first thing people say is, 'This doesn't look like a hospital,' which is one of the greatest compliments we hear." The quantity and quality of the services for patients and visitors help explain that reaction. Among them are a conference center, a museum, a multi-media learning center focused on health, a bank, a book store, three different restaurants, even a collection of retail establishments.

Consistent with its patient orientation, all inpatient rooms are private and large enough to accommodate visitors and staff. The angle of the windows allows more natural light and a better view. Though historically hospitals have frowned upon loved ones staying overnight with patients, Northwestern Memorial installed a pull-out bed to fit under the window seat. "More and more patients want family members to spend the night," Mecklenburg said, "and we encourage them to stay."

Understandably, one of patients' and staffs' greatest fears about inpatient stays is the all too frequent spread of infection. But Northwestern Memorial's state-of-the-art air-handling system works to eliminate that problem. In addition, sinks and surgical gloves are positioned in patients' rooms so that staff members, "can't get in or out of a room without washing their hands," observed Mecklenburg.

Explaining that "one of the ways you control costs is by best practices," he attributed the average patient length of stay, which is remarkably low for a teaching hospital (just over four days), to a reduction in complications like infections. "Our hospital's acquired infection rate is less than half the national average," according to Mecklenburg. "For example, our use of antibiotics is less than at comparable institutions. All of this raises quality and reduces cost."

It is still too early to conclude if Northwestern Memorial will continue to live up to Mecklenburg's predictions. Yet, his facility's investment in carefully designed physical assets (buildings) that meet patients' needs within the realities of contemporary healthcare may reflect its remedy to the dilemmas confronting hospitals in this country. In the process, Northwestern Memorial has created value with its buildings.

Northwestern Memorial is not the only organization using its real estate to its best advantage. Walgreen Company, based in Deerfield, Illinois, is also rich in land and buildings. The company, founded in 1901 as a 50-foot by 20-foot neighborhood drugstore has become the pharmacy all others are measured by and one of the most respected corporations in the United States. We will discuss how Walgreen creates value with all of its assets and relationships in Chapter 9, but here, our focus is on physical assets.

Who: Walgreen Company.
How: It focuses on convenience and access.

Walgreen's business model makes good use of traditional physical assets. It operates more than 3,300 drugstores in 43 states and Puerto Rico and plans to double that number in the next decade.

It is the nation's largest drugstore chain, and ranks fourteenth overall among retail companies. In fact, if measured according to average annual return on assets in the last 10 years, Walgreen even surpasses prosperous Wal-Mart Stores, Inc. — 9.34 percent versus 9.29 percent, respectively.

Key to the drug chain's success is its unwavering focus on convenience and accessibility for its target customers, defined as shoppers who visit pharmacies more than five times each month. The company has transformed its land and buildings into a busy shopper's one-stop, time-saving paradise. In so doing, it derives continuously growing value from these physical assets.

Not found in strip malls or shopping centers, Walgreen's new stores blanket selected markets with freestanding buildings that are usually located at the intersections of major streets and highways. That way, they are easy to find and can offer parking immediately adjacent to its stores.

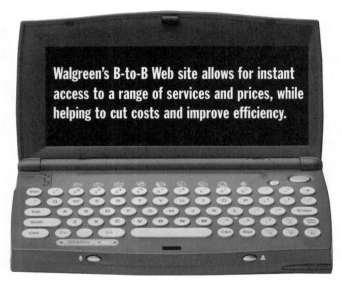

Walgreen's B-to-B Web site allows for instant access to a range of services and prices, while helping to cut costs and improve efficiency.

The store buildings themselves are designed to move shoppers through quickly. Two- thirds have drive-through windows for dropping off and picking up prescriptions. In all stores, direction signs are easy to spot and understand. Scanner-based checkouts — speed customers through the lines.

That it is rapidly opening new stores does not hinder Walgreen's efforts to maintain and renovate its older locations. It frequently updates fixtures, widens aisles, improves lighting, and brightens wall colors. Walgreen's dedication to creating value from its buildings is reflected in its motto: The store is the product.

Equipment.

Other important physical assets, in addition to real estate and buildings, are used by the healthcare industry to create value. In fact, every healthcare organization needs tools and instruments to function, such as laboratory test tubes and x-ray machines. The cost of the equipment, which shows up as an asset on the balance sheet, is written off over time. A healthcare enterprise can create value with these assets in a variety of ways.

"Between the years 2000 and 2010,
we're going to add another 3,000 stores.
We'll go from 3,000 stores to 6,000 stores
in 10 years. The new battle cry is,
'6 by 10.' . . . We're in the greatest
expansion period of our nearly 100-year history."

— L. Daniel Jorndt, *chairman, and chief executive officer, Walgreen Company.*

Equipment is a machine or tool used to undertake a specific task, say, a Walgreen checkout scanner. We include computer hardware in our definition, but not the codified knowledge embedded in computer software and systems, which we classify as an organization asset. Rite Aid Corporation is our case in point.

Who: Rite Aid Corporation.
How: It uses robots to boost efficiency.

Based in Camp Hill, Pennsylvania, Rite Aid is the nation's third largest drugstore chain and is known for its proficiency in using equipment to advance its business model.

Rite Aid had Rapid Script robotic dispensers in 870 of its 3,800 neighborhood stores at the end of 2000. Does this mean that a character like *Star Wars'* R2D2 will be filling your prescription? Not yet.

The Rite Aid system depends on technology developed by ScriptPro USA, Inc., in Mission, Kansas. As ScriptPro describes the process, a Rite Aid employee enters a doctor's prescription into a pharmacy computer that forwards it to a ScriptPro SP 200 dispensing system. The SP 200 uses a computer-controlled robotic arm to automatically select the designated drug and the correct vial. Then it counts out the prescribed number of pills into the container, applies a label, and delivers it uncapped to the pharmacist for verification and closure. Besides slashing the time required to fill a prescription, robotic dispensing also provides safeguards against human error. ScriptPro claims its equipment saves as much as two-thirds of manual dispensing costs, while speeding work flow and increasing accuracy.

Inventory.

No company operates with buildings and equipment alone. Inventory also plays an important role in the success of organizations. In a hospital gift shop, for example, the goods that are sold in the ordinary course of business — perfume, pens, cards, and flowers — comprise part of its inventory. The chemicals used to produce a pharmaceutical maker's medication are also part of its inventory, as are the pills that pharmacists dispense to patients.

To be more specific, we return to Walgreen for a closer look at how a company can use inventory to create value.

Who: Walgreen Company.
How: It manages its inventory.

Though we've said it before, that Walgreen has 3,300 stores and plans for an additional 3,000 before 2010 deserves repeating. It goes without saying that inventory is an enormous asset that this company intends to preserve by applying technology — specifically, its Strategic Inventory Management System (SIMS).

SIMS cost the company $60 million when it was developed in the late 1980s and early 1990s to reduce inventory spending and improve in-stock performance. But it has paid for itself many times over. To date, the system has saved the company more than $1 billion in warehouse inventory expenses, and that number grows as Walgreen expands.

How does it work? SIMS is an automated system that keeps Walgreen's massive distribution centers moving their inventory out the doors and into the stores. Up-to-the-minute information technology keeps track of exactly what is moving off the shelves at each store so that goods can be replaced almost instantly. Walgreen is one of only a handful of drug chains that manages inventory at the store level.

Prior to SIMS' implementation, all Walgreen orders were processed at a single location. This meant that in the case of disaster or any prolonged loss of power, nothing moved from warehouses to stores. Now, each distribution center has its own processing center, and individual stores are connected to them by satellite. Order requests are automatically determined from in-store purchase data and forwarded to the appropriate distribution center.

Inside its warehouses, Walgreen is using its equipment assets to move and manage inventory with automated product-picking technology. One system, called Pick to Light, quickly directs warehouse employees to the product they need to access first as they fill an order.

Driverless vehicles are another of Walgreen's innovations that quickly and efficiently transport items around the warehouses.

"... the phrase 'our tools become us'

has two meanings. Even as we develop devices

and systems that make us smarter,

faster, stronger, more beautiful,

and perhaps even immortal, in other laboratories

around the world a competing race

is being constructed. There, brilliant computers,

clever chips, and autonomic robots are being built,

not just to imitate but to succeed us.

Cyborgs await us in the future with skeletons

a thousand times as sturdy as ours,

nerves a billion times as quick,

eyes that can see a flower a mile away

in all of the colors of the electromagnetic

spectrum, and flesh that will shiver

at the touch of a single snowflake."

— *Forbes ASAP.*

Elsewhere in its warehouses, automated sorting systems keep products for outbound shipments speeding by at a rate of 5,000 to 6,500 per hour. The system actually has the capability of sorting 9,000 packages per hour during peak times. When asked if this technology is aimed at reducing the number of employees, Walgreen managers reply with an emphatic "no." The whole point is to make sure shipments aren't held up and stores aren't left with empty shelves.

As we explained earlier, by managing its inventory assets, Walgreen is ensuring that its shelf space will continue to provide optimum value to its primary customers.

▶ What's Next?

In Chapter 5, we show that a broad range of healthcare organizations can and do extract enormous value from their financial assets.

Questions to ask yourself.

Business Model: Does your healthcare company acquire and manage the right combination of physical assets in order to create value? Consider each of the primary physical assets: land, buildings, inventory, and equipment.

Risk: Think of the healthcare companies you know well, including competitors, suppliers, and strategic partners. Do any excel at taking risks as they purchase, refurbish, or dispose of physical assets in order to create value? How does your company rate against these organizations?

Technology: Do the case studies presented in this chapter suggest ways that your company might use the latest technologies (the Internet and e-commerce) to connect and enhance all your assets and relationships?

Measurement: What are your industry's best practices for managing physical assets? Are they properly measured to insure your future success? Do they enable you to make interim course corrections so that as your circumstances change, your company's physical assets continue to create value and avoid destroying it?

5 WHO'S CREATING VALUE WITH FINANCIAL ASSETS?

Many business decisions are predicated upon balance-sheet numbers. And many of those decisions are ill-informed, because financial assets represent only one piece of the puzzle.

*"... cash and coin notwithstanding, money itself
is merely an agreed-upon representation
of that other great ... truth: value.
And I can assure you, value is real."*
— Scott McNealy, *cofounder, chairman, and chief executive officer,
Sun Microsystems, Inc.*

The turmoil in the healthcare industry is forcing all those working in it — physicians, hospital administrators, insurers — to redefine their goals and rethink their financial assets, that is, their capital resources.

Unlike other industries, healthcare is by its very mission, dedicated to the health and well-being of its ultimate customer, the patient — a customer by all other industry definitions. This humanitarian emphasis doesn't gainsay the reality that healthcare organizations are businesses that sell products and services. Like companies in any other industry, they must earn at least enough to support themselves. In most cases, they must also reward their investors or, at the very least, pay back their loans. This tension is often cast in the "either/or" conundrum of margin versus mission in healthcare.

Sister Irene Kraus, the former president of the Daughters of Charity National Health System (DCNHS), based in St. Louis, Missouri, expressed this dilemma most succinctly: "No margin, no mission." Sister Irene's experience on the subject is formidable. During her time at the helm, no healthcare organization had a better financial record than the coast-to-coast network run by the Roman Catholic order called Daughters of Charity.

In addition to its 49 hospitals and numerous freestanding treatment facilities in a dozen states, the system operated nursing schools, as well. The order maintained rigorous financial control of its institutions and was willing to exit a market if it could not sustain its mission through successful financial performance.

In 1998, the system posted net income of $244 million on revenues of $4 billion, with a portfolio of $2 billion in investments and cash. This was achieved while continuing to provide $266 million dollars of care for the poor. Yet, despite its financial sophistication, legerdemain, and enormous success in aligning mission with margin, in 1999, the Daughters of Charity organization merged its health system with the Sisters of St. Joseph Health System, based in Ann Arbor, Michigan. In so doing, they jointly created a co-sponsorship model named Ascension Health, the largest not-for-profit healthcare provider in the country.

In the following pages, we discuss the tumultuous process by which the Daughters of Charity redesigned its business model to make the most of its financial assets in the context of today's changed economic environment and, ultimately, decided to join forces with another compatible healthcare institution.

For more than a century, the Daughters has demonstrated prudence and creativity. In the early 1980s, the order recognized the benefit of organizing its community-based hospitals across the country into a national system. It led the Catholic healthcare industry and much of the broader industry toward a national approach to key activities, such as purchasing, pension plan management, and financial practices. It established cash-investment and debt-management programs that became models within the industry. In the early 1990s, when other hospital systems began to merge with unprecedented frequency, DCNHS remained independent. It recognized the powerful economic forces pushing hospitals into mergers, joint operating agreements, and other partnership models, but felt no need to pursue these strategies because the order's operating performance was strong.

However, in the spring of 1997, DCNHS leveraged its financial resources to float a bond offering. The goal was to refinance existing debt as well as finance capital expenditures. Two other healthcare systems — Baptist/St. Vincent's Health System, in Jacksonville, Florida, and Western Maryland Health System, in Cumberland, Maryland — joined the expanded obligated group as full partners. The result was $862.4 million in total financing.

The two outside systems pledged to match the debt- and credit-rating standards set for the original group members, all of which were hospitals owned by DCNHS. The fully and easily subscribed offering was a major step in the order's effort to connect with other nonprofit systems. The transactions moved smoothly because of the Daughters' strong financial position and savvy methods of procuring and making the most of those assets.

"Life is like a coin. You can spend it any way you wish, but you can only spend it once."

— Miguel de Cervantes.

Jerry Widman, senior vice president of finance for DCNHS, notes that it was the first time DCNHS had other units with which it had to consult and make decisions. "Instead of single hospitals going to the market, a larger entity can go within a short time interval," Widman pointed out. "Thus, you get lower interest rates because of a better credit rating, and that tends to provide better access to capital."

If DCNHS were involved, financing a bond transaction would cost less than 1 percent of proceeds; for freestanding hospitals, the ante was 1.5 percent to 2 percent of proceeds. On a billion-dollar deal, such savings can reach tens of millions of dollars. With its obligated group offering, DCNHS moved toward its goal.

In 1999, the Daughters of Charity and the Sisters of St. Joseph decided jointly that Catholic healthcare could be strengthened through the successful "co-sponsorship" of a larger health system and the two orders merged to create Ascension Health. It boasts a network of over 75 acute- and long-term beds, and other healthcare facilities in 15 states and the District of Columbia. It is also the largest Catholic health system in the United States, and employs over 87,000 people.

While the economic challenges in the healthcare industry have caused many downgrades and unstable ratings, the Daughters of Charity has maintained a double-A credit rating on all of the bonds it has issued since 1983. So has Ascension Health.

In every way, the achievements of the Daughters of Charity have defied the widely believed notion that mission and margin cannot peacefully coexist. The good news is that other healthcare organizations are also building business models that make the most of their financial assets to create value. In this chapter, we show how.

Financial assets include, as one might expect, cash and receivables, investments, debt, and equity. They also determine a company's financial status and its ability to borrow capital and attract investors.

For example, cash plays an important role in any economy or, for that matter, in any company. At the end of the day, we measure our success by our ability to collect more cash than we pay out. Cash is the term for ready money — what Lord Byron referred to in *Don Juan* as "Aladdin's Lamp." In short, it is, literally, the currency of business, the lifeblood of your enterprise, whether it be a dot.com or a bricks-and-mortar company.

Awaited cash is known as a receivable. Receivables are claims that a business has from its customers for the sale of goods or services. For instance, the pharmacy's bill to a nursing facility for prescriptions administered to patients, or the invoice from the home-healthcare agency that provided nurses to assist a post-surgical patient. Though receivables represent promises by customers or partners to pay, the balance sheet acknowledges the possibility that those promises will not be realized, and they are labeled doubtful accounts.

Managing cash and receivables is more difficult and also more rewarding than it may sound. The same is true for managing investments and equity, as the remainder of this chapter shows.

Investments.

Though the term investor may evoke images of individuals or day traders glued to computer screens, our focus is elsewhere — on the cor-

The corporate investor—the corporation that uses its portfolio to reap significant returns and create extraordinary value by investing in the financial instruments of other companies.

poration that uses its portfolio to reap significant returns and create value by investing in the financial instruments of other companies. The corporate investor, like the individual one, is interested in the securities of other companies when it perceives the promise of a significant return. Although one business may invest in another to gain control of it, our concern is with those minority investments that are intended to create value in the long term. Common stocks, bonds, and other financial instruments fall into this category.

To understand the implications of this type of asset investment, we will again visit Northwestern Memorial Health Care. In Chapter 4, we pointed out the unusual financial status of this Chicago institution, a vigorous, thriving not-for-profit healthcare facility with plenty of money in its coffers. In this chapter, we consider that organization in another context.

Who: Northwestern Memorial Health Care.
How: It invests wisely.

Even before it opened its new 2-million-square-foot downtown hospital in the spring of 1999 (on time and under budget), Northwestern Memorial easily met its interest payments on the loans it took out to construct the new state-of-the-art facility. It is the largest privately funded building project in Illinois, and it was financed with just 40 percent debt.

Northwestern Memorial managed that feat by achieving an operating profit margin of 11.6 percent — a full 8.8 percentage points higher than the national average of 2.8 percent for major teaching hospitals. It also has $1 billion in highly profitable liquid investments. In fact, more than half of the $580 million used to build the new hospital came from its return on investments in the stock and bond markets, combined with savings from cost-cutting programs.

Unlike its traditional, more conservative counterparts, the hospital's parent, Northwestern Memorial Health Care, has not shied away from actively investing non-operating assets in domestic and international equities. They yielded the company net returns of 26.5 percent in 1995, 16.1 percent in 1996, and 19.9 percent in 1997.

Eugene Principi, Northwestern Memorial Health Care's treasurer and senior vice president of finance, noted not long ago that the hospital's investments "helped us get our cash reserves much sooner than anticipated." By using its investment earnings to finance the construction, the hospital is reaching healthcare utopia: Growth through expanded services without draining operating income.

Northwestern Memorial exemplifies our contention that maximum value is created for your company when you make the most of all of your assets. And this is true even if your business model focuses primarily on only one or two asset categories.

Equity.

If you aim to succeed in the global financial markets, your ability to build equity in the markets has never been as crucial as it is right now. In a time of ceaseless change, intense competition, and ever-improving technology, corporations must be ready to take large risks to protect and increase the value of their assets. The markets allow them to disperse that risk over many investors, making it easier to generate the funds required to compete.

Making money by investing in one's own stock is nothing new in today's economy. In fact, Dell Computer Corporation makes more money playing the stock market than it does selling computers. Over a three-year period, Dell earned a notable $2.5 billion and an even more impressive $3.1 billion in stock-market gains.

Some of today's biggest winners, such as Dell, Intel Corporation, and Microsoft Corporation are masters of a stock-market strategy called calls and puts. How does this potentially lucrative strategy work?

Dell, Intel, Microsoft, or any other company with a hot stock can bet on its own continued success by buying calls and puts. In the first option, buying calls, the purchaser is allowed to buy stock at a certain price before a specified date. In the second, the purchaser of puts has the right to sell stock at a certain price before a designated expiration date.

The person who buys a Dell put is betting that the stock will go down, while the buyer of a call is taking the opposite side of the wager. In our example, Dell, itself, is the call purchaser. When the stock goes up, as Dell's stock did for nearly four years, Dell collects the cash from all the expired puts.

Amgen, Inc., based in Thousand Oaks, California, is making money from its stock, but with a slightly different method.

> ## If you aim to succeed in the global financial markets, your ability to build equity in the markets has never been as crucial as it is right now.

Who: Amgen, Inc.
How: It invests in itself through stock buybacks.

It is the largest and most successful biotechnology company in the world. Its major product, Epogen, which treats patients diagnosed with end-stage kidney disease, is in fourth place among the top-selling prescription drugs in the United States.

As other healthcare companies rush into mergers or acquisitions, Amgen is creating value in what has, so far, been a less risky and more rewarding fashion: It is buying its own stock. The buyback program is immense. In 1998, the company retrieved 54 million shares worth $912 million and, in 1999, another 27.1 million shares worth $1.02 billion. Amgen has authorized the purchase of another $2 billion worth of its stock by December 31, 2002. With the steady rise in the price of Amgen stock — from $26.14 a share at the close of 1998 to $63.94 at the close of 2000 — the company has realized a significant gain on its buybacks. True, an acquisition or merger might have realized that kind of value, but it is far less likely given the high rate of failures of business combinations.

Amgen, like other companies in this chapter, is using more than its financial assets to create value. For example, it is exploiting its intellectual property, an organization asset that is critical to the success of any biotechnology company, and one we will discuss further in Chapter 8.

Amgen, Inc., was founded with an $80,000 venture-capital loan.

▶ What's Next?

Until now, we have concentrated on traditional tangible assets. In the chapters that follow, we move to the intangible side, showing how organization assets and relationships with employees, suppliers, and customers can create value for your organization. These assets and relationships do not appear on the balance sheet, of course. But they must be considered by any health-care organization that wants to achieve success in today's fast-changing economic environment.

In Chapter 6, we show how some healthcare companies are already using employee and supplier assets to create value.

Questions to ask yourself.

Business Model: Think of your organization's financial assets. Are you effectively creating, managing, and investing these assets to create value, or are you allowing them to sit idly? Look at industries outside your own and see what the best companies are doing. Are there any lessons there for you?

Risk: How does your company invest in and create a proprietary portfolio of financial assets that contributes to its business model? Consider cash, receivables, investments, debt, and equity as sources of value creation. Ask yourself if your company is taking appropriate risks with its assets. Is it making the mistake of trying to avoid risk altogether?

Technology: Do the case studies in this chapter suggest ways that you could change how your company manages its financial assets? Might you be creating additional value by installing new technologies that would allow you to make more informed decisions?

Measurement: What are the healthcare industry's best practices for managing financial assets? Are these standards properly measuring the myriad ways your financial assets can be exploited, or just the traditional ways?

6 WHO'S CREATING VALUE WITH EMPLOYEES AND SUPPLIERS?

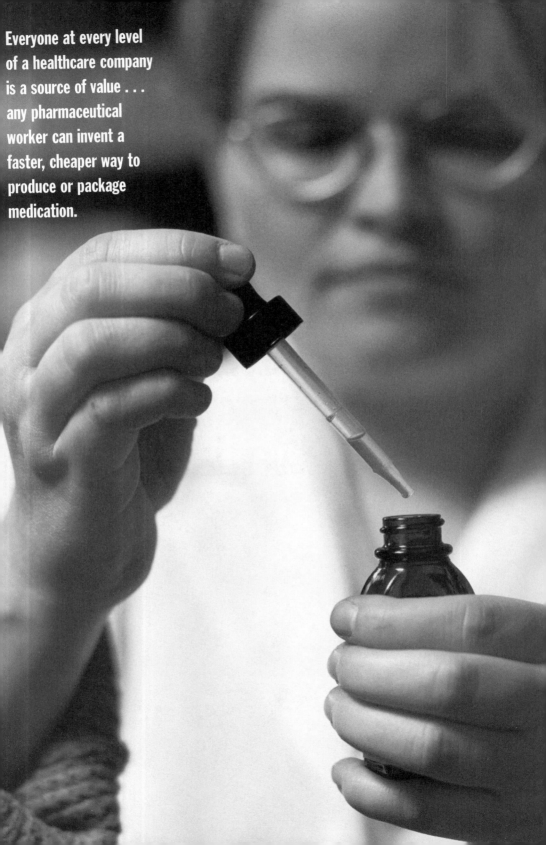

Everyone at every level of a healthcare company is a source of value . . . any pharmaceutical worker can invent a faster, cheaper way to produce or package medication.

"An organization, no matter how well designed, is only as good as the people who live and work in it."
— Dee W. Hock,
founder and chief executive officer emeritus, Visa International, Inc.

In the early 1980s, the director of a residency program in family medicine in a big city hospital addressed a new group of graduates. "You have a choice," he said.

"You can either sign your checks on the front or the back. If you are salaried, your employer obviously gives you a check, and you sign it on the back. If you own your practice, though, you have the freedom to write your own checks and sign them on the front."

Then, he added with a chuckle: "Of course, that way, you are also choosing to spend your own money."

In those days, the vast majority of doctors chose to become small-business owners, signing the front of the check to pay employees and suppliers.

Today, where managed care reigns, more and more physicians are signing their checks on the back. They are salaried employees of hospitals and insurance companies. So it is that doctors, in their dual roles, embody two of the sources of value in the Value Dynamics category that we call employees and suppliers.

As we pointed out earlier, traditional measurement and management systems take into account only tangible assets in two basic categories: physical assets such as land, equipment, and inventory; and financial assets, such as investments, cash, and accounts receivable. The remaining sources of value are overlooked or mistakenly categorized.

Throughout the United States, companies — including those in healthcare — are in a war for talent, competing furiously for the best and the brightest people with little thought as to how that talent should most accurately be measured. Instead, they continue, erroneously, to measure and manage employees and suppliers as expenses — that is, as unpredictable and costly expenditures that diminish quarterly earnings and reduce the value of a business.

In this chapter, however, we use Value Dynamics as a new context in which to consider relationships with employees, suppliers, and partners — as assets. And we show how managers at some leading healthcare organizations have created value with these assets.

Employees.

Bernie Marcus, chairman and co-founder of do-it-yourself retailer, The Home Depot, Inc., is quick to credit his company's employees for the organization's success. "You get what you pay for," he likes to say. "If you pay . . . minimum wage, [employees] aren't . . . motivated to learn anything or to take care of that customer." His enthusiasm for his employees translates into market share: Home Depot commands an estimated 30 percent of the $200-billion-a-year U.S. home-improvement and building- materials market.

> "Chief executives have always talked about the importance of their people but now it's for real because it's financial."
>
> —Charles Handy, *The Hungry Spirit.*

Stanley Sword, who carries the title of chief people officer at Cerner Corporation, a Kansas City, Missouri-based producer of software for the healthcare industry, has a novel view of employees as volunteers, who decide every day whether they are going to come to work. Given the competition for highly qualified technology personnel in the healthcare industry, Sword suggests that a company must use every means possible to get its people into the office each day. That calls for strategies and programs aimed at recruiting and retaining the "volunteers." As Sword sees it, his job is "to create a work environment that positions Cerner as the place to be for information-technology professionals who want to work in healthcare."

Who: Cerner Corporation.
How: It rewards its people with stock options.

Cerner entices prospective new hires with signing bonuses and stock options. In addition, the company rewards current employees who attract new ones. A Cerner employee can earn between $1,500 and $5,000 for each person the company hires based on his or her recommendation. As Stan Sword knows, companies prosper when employees devote their experience, skill, and enthusiasm to their jobs.

In our view, virtually everyone at every level of a healthcare company is a source of value, including part- and full-time employees, contingent workers, and independent contractors. Arbitrary standards for determining who is and is not an employee have no place in this category. Position, tenure, or salary level in the corporate hierarchy aren't relevant to an employee's value. The newest nurse may devise a less painful way to care for burn victims; the lowest ranking pharmaceutical line worker may invent a faster, less expensive way to produce and package pills.

The late Walt Disney understood the point. When he was completing Disneyland, he asked everyone — from electricians to executives — to test each ride. Though the practice seemed far-fetched to many, it was actually quite astute. As it turned out, something was wrong with one of his attractions — "The Pirates of the Caribbean." After a construction worker took a ride, he told Disney that something was wrong, but he didn't know what. "Ride it again," Disney responded, then added, characteristically, "and keep on riding it until you've figured it out." The construction worker did just that, finally realizing that what was missing in this reproduction of the Caribbean fantasy was fireflies. Soon, fireflies were blinking throughout the ride.

Cerner, Disney, and Home Depot are not the only companies that have recognized the flaw in our conventional measurement and management systems. Pharmaceutical giant Merck & Company, Inc., is another.

Who: Merck & Company, Inc.
How: It treats its employees like customers.

Merck, the world's largest pharmaceutical maker, structures its business model around its employees, and that strategy has paid off handsomely in innovations. Typically, Merck's winning ideas emerge from a research-and-development process to which millions of work hours and hundreds of millions of dollars are dedicated annually to the hunt for a drug breakthrough — or even a reformulation of an old drug. Sometimes, though, the breakthrough comes not from the research-and-development process itself, but from the mind of a single, inspired and motivated employee. That happens because Merck knows how to value its employees as sources of value, not expenses.

Just such a breakthrough occurred some time ago as Merck was developing a new formulation of Fosamax. This drug is widely used to treat osteoporosis, a degenerative bone disease that particularly targets post-menopausal women. It is prescribed to be taken daily, but an employee had a hunch that it might be just as effective if administered in a weekly dose. In all likelihood, his hunch will provide Merck's osteoporosis drug with an advantage over its daily-dose competitors.

Drugs for chronic conditions are almost always taken at least once a day to maintain an elevated level of the substance in the bloodstream. If you miss a single dose, you impair the effectiveness of the entire treatment. But as anyone on a drug regimen knows, it is almost impossible to remember to take a medicine at the same time each day, particularly when that regimen is for life, and especially if that drug is not the only one the patient takes regularly.

Until this Merck employee thought about it, no one ques-

"When the partially constructed Virginia plant for Merck's new AIDS drug, Crixivan, got buried under four feet of snow, everyone from managers to lab workers rushed in with snow shovels. That helped Merck get the lifesaving drug off the production line just 15 months after breaking ground, 9 months ahead of schedule. You won't find a column measuring that kind of dedication and resourcefulness on any kind of balance sheet."

— *Business Week.*

tioned whether Fosamax required such frequent doses. As it happened, the osteoporosis medication binds to the bone, making its useful life much longer than that of many other drugs. Thus, this medicine offers patients convenience, lower costs, and, perhaps, significant clinical advantage. In the excruciatingly competitive pharmaceuticals industry, even the tiniest variation between drugs can make the difference between a winner and a flop.

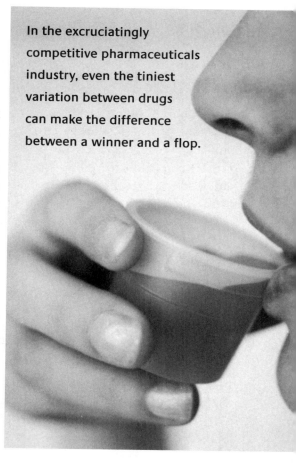

In the excruciatingly competitive pharmaceuticals industry, even the tiniest variation between drugs can make the difference between a winner and a flop.

Merck is leading the way in today's economy because it recognizes each of its employees as a source of value — and because it has found ways to maintain its relationships with employees in the extremely competitive job market.

The company's appreciation of its employees is shown in large and small ways. As a Merck employee, you may find your errands have been run, your car serviced, and your dry cleaning picked up. More importantly, the company provides on-site childcare, health and fitness services, free medical screenings, and routine healthcare. Such treatment only makes sense since Merck attributes the lines of medications that define its success directly to its employees' creativity and loyalty.

Guidant Corporation is another organization that works aggressively to support the health and well-being of its employees and has done so since it began in 1994 as a spin-off of Eli Lilly & Company.

Who: Guidant Corporation.
How: It promotes employee health and development.

Elaborate in-house gymnasiums and exercise programs are just the beginning of the facilities and programs available to the employees of Guidant, a world-leading manufacturer of devices used in the treatment of heart and artery disorders. Based in Indianapolis, Indiana, the company also sponsors programs to help workers quit smoking and reimburses the program fees for all who succeed.

The increased awareness of cardiovascular disease is a motivating factor for both company and employees. On the subject of the anti-smoking campaign, for example, Katherine Mathews, a Guidant manager, commented, "We don't want to produce our own patients."

Guidant's commitment to the well-being and satisfaction of its employees takes many forms, including educational and training programs, a work environment that is both considerate and supportive, and stock options. All of these benefits represent the company's efforts to create value with its employees.

The tone is set from the top by the president and chief executive officer, Ron Dollens, who is well aware that innovation has been — and will be — essential to Guidant's success in the medical-device industry. (Some 64 percent of his company's revenues at any one time are derived from products created in the previous six months.) He is equally aware that every one of his 6,000 employees, not only the scientists, is instrumental to keeping the new-product pipeline full.

Dollens has fostered a company-wide culture of positive reinforcement that keeps his people motivated. "Celebrate what you want to see more of," he tells his managers, to whom he gives generous latitude in their operating decisions, and expects them to do the same with their workers. "We have to let others get the same level of fulfillment we have through our company's successes, so they have high levels of involvement," explained Dollens. In support of that position, the chief executive insists upon cultivating and promoting employees to higher posts, rather than hiring from outside the company. He uses outside consultants to challenge static assumptions and provide new perspectives.

Guidant promotes loyalty, too, by making it easy for workers to accumulate company stock. In one retirement plan, employees automatically receive shares of stock equal to 5 percent of their monthly base pay. In another savings plan, each employee dollar is matched with 50 cents in company stock. There is also an annual bonus paid in stock options for all employees.

To personalize all of this, Guidant offers seminars that explain stock ownership and the relationship between a stock's value and the performance of the company's employees. Also, programs have been established to help Guidant's people develop their potential in areas that include computer skills, manufacturing processes, and marketing through in-house and outside educational programs. Full tuition is provided for approved college courses. Meanwhile, together with their managers, employees develop individualized plans intended to round out their skills and experience; the plans might call for special coaching or rotating assignments.

Establishing the tone of civility and teamwork he seeks for his company, Dollens spends most of his week making the rounds of Guidant's 44 offices and meeting employees. "When he walks through the hallway at any one of our sites in the world," an executive noted, "he knows people by name, he knows their family's names, and recalls past experiences with them."

It is typical of Dollens' emphasis on mutual respect and the importance of family life that he will postpone a meeting from a Monday until Tuesday so that an attendee will not have to travel on a weekend. Time spent with their families, he believes, puts workers in a better frame of mind to perform on the job. Dollens' sensitivity would have been considered unnecessary and, indeed, counterproductive just 50 years ago. Fortunately, he and many other leaders of today's economy have recognized that it is necessary for productivity.

Creating an atmosphere of mutual respect and involvement, Guidant has earned record sales and profits by giving its employees a personal stake in the company's success. This clearly demonstrates how a company can create great value with its employees.

Suppliers.

As companies' formerly rigid borders expand to become more inclusive and permeable in our newly interconnected economy, suppliers, like employees, are being recognized as sources of value. Indeed, outsourcing has made suppliers critical to nearly every company's success, despite the fact that they — like employees — are currently categorized as expenses.

Healthcare software provider Cerner is among the successful companies that understand the new reality: To steadily improve results, it cannot rely solely on its own people and their skills; it must look to outsiders for help producing what it calls "world-class products and services."

Cerner's Web site lists more than 15 suppliers, which provide the company with such products as network-management tools, client-server technology, pen-based personal computers, laser printers, bar-code printers, and secure Internet connections. Moreover, Cerner, itself, receives technical education, marketing assistance, and technical support from its suppliers so that it can aid its own clients.

In many healthcare organizations, suppliers have a low priority. With certain exceptions — notably, the insurance companies that provide corporations with their benefits packages — suppliers are primarily chosen based on their price. Years ago, the Japanese automobile industry revealed how misguided this limited view can be. By establishing long-term, close relationships with selected suppliers, Toyota Motor Corporation was able to enlist suppliers in improving both its product and its production efficiency. In the end, the car maker, aided by its suppliers, was so successful at cutting costs and increasing product quality that its vehicles were in demand worldwide. Subsequently, the entire auto industry embraced Toyota's method.

With some adjustments, supplies can play a comparable role in the healthcare industry. Companies need to select and retain suppliers not just on the basis of price but on quality and dedication. There must be strong, mutually beneficial relationships with suppliers if the two parties are to create value together.

Another organization that has created value with suppliers is medibuy, Inc.

Who: medibuy, Inc.
How: It connects its customers with its suppliers.

Thousands of hospitals, nursing homes, physicians, pharmacies, and rehabilitation centers, as well as government health facilities regularly sign on to medibuy.com in search of the best prices for their purchases. Manufacturers, dealers, and distributors visit the site hoping to find the best value in everything: medical devices and equipment, maintenance supplies, computers, even office supplies.

"Celebrate what you want to see more of."

— Ron Dollens, *president and chief executive officer, Guidant Corporation.*

In essence, medibuy creates value for itself by making it possible for other companies to create value for themselves through the suppliers represented on the Web site. For medibuy, those suppliers translate into sources of value that pay a fee for each completed online transaction.

For buyer and seller alike, medibuy offers major savings. The marketplace for medical supplies today is about $300 billion, and medibuy says it is saving businesses almost $11 billion a year in processing costs.

The company offers visitors a choice from four separate services:

The most familiar is called *Catalog,* which is, as its name suggests, a click-and-buy online catalog. It offers an array of medical supplies, equipment, and services from a growing community of suppliers. The information provided through *Catalog* is electronically linked with suppliers' databases, ensuring accurate, real-time supplier pricing and immediate access to available inventory information. It also coordinates buyer-specific pricing and specific pre-negotiated contract pricing.

At *Auction,* **buyers and sellers can make bids** and sell their used equipment or disposable inventory.

Excess inventory and promotional items can also be found at *Specials,* along with promotional items. The goods are posted at deep discounts for a limited amount of time.

At *RFP,* **medibuy welcomes proposals from buyers** for any and every kind of medical supply and piece of equipment. Bids are seen only by the buyer.

For suppliers, medibuy has many attractions. In addition to opening access to a new world of potential buyers, the site makes it possible to keep the data and pricing of their products constantly updated. It also lets them cut the cost of processing orders with current customers.

Gary Wagner, a materials-management vice president, described his purchase from medibuy of $15 million in linens for his employer, Inova Health System, in Springfield, Virginia: "We saved 18 percent on acquisition costs. It's that kind of opportunity that is drawing so many to check with medibuy."

Today, in unprecedented fashion, healthcare organizations are forming partnerships that will extend the reach and richness of their business models.

Gary Weston is the director of material services for Banner Health, Colorado, a division of Banner Health Systems, a network of four hospitals based in Greeley, Colorado. When negotiating prices of goods he wants to buy, Weston will sometimes use the medibuy approach. Unless the sales representative comes up with a lower bid, Weston warns, he will put a request for proposal (RFP) on that particular industry's business-to-business Web site. Faced with the prospect of having to bid against a whole industry of competitors, the sales representative tends to offer a better price.

What medibuy has accomplished is remarkable even though, in some ways, it mimics how marketplace entrepreneurs have conducted business for centuries. Like sponsors of trade shows and industry fairs, the company has provided an environment where buyers and sellers can conveniently do business. Generally, those earlier sponsors made their profits by renting out space, while medibuy receives a fee for each transaction, but the underlying goal is the same: to create value from suppliers — even when the suppliers are actually selling their wares to somebody else.

Partners.

The third source of value in the employee and supplier category assets is relationships with partners. We define partners as two or more individuals or organizations that jointly control the economic activities of an enterprise.

Today, in unprecedented fashion, healthcare organizations are forming partnerships that will extend the reach and richness of their business models. For example, global pharmaceutical companies are seeking partners (from biotechnology companies to retailers, and even to customers directly). Sought to strengthen the pharmaceutical companies' knowledge base and enhance their access to new markets, these relationships offer exposure, which, in turn, helps them gain global market share. We see this phenomenon across the entire economy as organizations become increasingly permeable, relying to a growing extent on their supply chains and outsourcing partners at one end, and distributors at the other.

Partners make it possible for organizations not only to augment the services and products they offer customers, but also to expand geographically. Such growth may come through brick-and-mortar distribution systems or through the Internet, though a third option will soon be available: mobile commerce. By defining relationships with partners as sources of value, we emphasize that an organization's sources of value are both owned and unowned, inside the organization and external to it. One Independent Practice Association (IPA) we know had a serious problem that it solved through an interesting arrangement in partnering.

Who: An Independent Practice Association.
How: It's partners are its competitors, and vice versa.

The IPA provides HMO members, physicians, hospitals, with managed-healthcare services. The group offers treatment for behavioral and mental disorders and a health-education program taught by experts in a variety of medical disciplines. This is in addition to the usual and expected primary and specialty physician services.

A major limitation on the group's growth was the fact that the 37 people assigned to enter insurance claims into databases could type only 150 paper insurance claims a day, and the claims were pouring in at the rate of 200,000 a month. The data-entry employees had to wade through giant manuals to determine whether individual claims should be approved or denied.

Then, WebMD Corporation came to the rescue. The Atlanta, Georgia-based company, which started out in 1996 as Healtheon, was a brainchild of James Clark, the entrepreneurial genius whose previous ventures included Silicon Graphics, Inc. and Netscape Communications Corporation. Clark's plan was to harness the power of the computer and the Internet for the purpose of renovating the healthcare industry from the inside out and preparing it to cope with the challenges of the information revolution.

Initially, Healtheon was mired in prosaic matters, automating transactions and other back-office operations, but eventually Clark found a partner, WebMD: a young, increasingly popular Internet portal that supplied the public in general, and doctors in particular, with medical information.

"The quality of customer experience a partner delivers is the single most important criterion in our selection process. We simply won't build a partnership with any company that does not share our passion for serving customers."

— Jeffrey P. Bezos, *founder, chairman, and chief executive officer, Amazon.com, Inc.*

The theory was this: At the WebMD site, patients and healthcare professionals — doctors, nurses, pharmacists, and administrators — would be able to interact as well as tap other major sources of advice. The merger of the two companies won a strong vote of confidence from investors, and now WebMD has alliances with a variety of healthcare organizations including CVS Corporation, the drugstore chain; Eli Lilly & Company, the drug manufacturer; and Humana, Inc., the giant managed-care network. In Value Dynamics terms, WebMD, in its alliances with several established organizations, has created new value with its partners.

WebMD formed another less ballyhooed alliance with the IPA. When the IPA heard about Clark's company, it sought the partnership for help with its overwhelming data entering problem. In 45 minutes, WebMD processes 3,500 claims. Remember, the IPA was entering 150 a day.

At the start of 2000, WebMD was processing one-third of the IPA's claims, and that percentage was expected to double by year's end. Nine of the IPA's claims-processing employees have been moved elsewhere. Like WebMD before it, the IPA is creating value with its partners.

▶ What's Next?

In the world beyond healthcare, companies often pride themselves on how close they come to meeting this clichéd goal: "The customer is always right." Many in the healthcare business are taking a somewhat different tack as they create business models today. In the next chapter, we discuss relationships with important sources of value. We also look at programs undertaken by healthcare companies that are seeking new ways to reach and sell to increasingly independent consumers.

Questions to ask yourself.

Business Model: Identify the full range of your organization's relationships with employees and suppliers, whether they are maintenance people, nurses, manufacturers, or systems integrators. Are you effectively managing these relationships to create value for your enterprise?

Risk: How does your company go about taking risks? Does it prefer to hire and control all of its employees and suppliers, or is it comfortable extending its supply chain to partnerships, alliances, subcontractors, and other, newer forms of relationships.

Technology: Do the case studies in this chapter suggest any ways that your company might use new technologies, systems, and processes to link together all of its employees and suppliers?

Measurement: How does your organization track and measure the value-creating contributions of employees, suppliers, and partners? Has this approach changed in recent years? Does it use the newest knowledge-management techniques to perform these measurements?

7 WHO'S CREATING VALUE WITH CUSTOMERS?

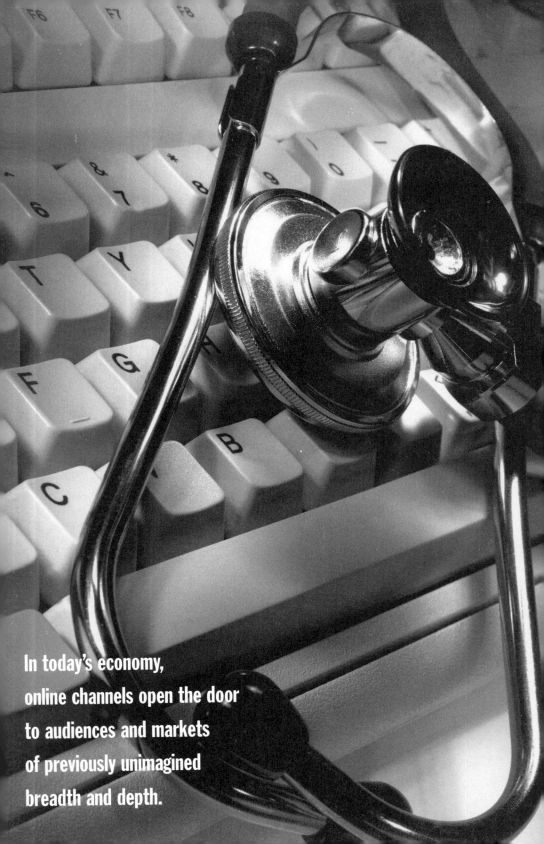

In today's economy,
online channels open the door
to audiences and markets
of previously unimagined
breadth and depth.

*"There's a revolution underway in healthcare,
and it's not the revolution you read about in the newspaper. . . .
The real revolution in healthcare is the patient revolution."*
— William W. George, *chairman and chief executive officer, Medtronic, Inc.*

Question:
Who's in the healthcare business?

America Online is, for one. If you log onto AOL, the most popular of all U.S. online services, you will find a panel labeled "health." Click on the panel and you come to a page jammed with links to a plethora of health-care information. You can visit allhealth.com, where one recent topic was PMS. Or, you can click on to Intelihealth.com, a subsidiary of Aetna U.S. Healthcare, where the question of the day was "Who's Getting the Flu?" The focus was the Great American Smoke Out, and the advertisers included Nicorette gum.

You can also access HealthCompass, a service established by HealthMagic, Inc., where you can maintain, receive, and distribute personal health information on yourself and your family. You control access to your information on the site, including your confidential

"Lifelong Health Record." The Web site has the capacity to hold everything from laboratory and diagnostic tests results to data on your medications, such as their side effects.

Yet, as things now stand, doctors, insurers, and hospitals exchange a motley array of data with no common standard of communication. The need for an online company that will coordinate, organize, and disburse this information (as well as the potential profits it is likely to earn) are clear. Estimates are that $200 billion a year is spent on healthcare administration that relies on various paper-based systems and outdated information technology.

Although everyone agrees that fragmented information systems are serving no one well — not patients, doctors, employers, or insurers — the task of connecting the systems with each other poses enormous problems, not the least of which is security. The system must be available at all times, while the very private nature of the data demands an invulnerable security system.

Connectivity is the key to unleashing the promise of the healthcare industry, and the major focus of that connectivity must be on the customer, a.k.a. the patient. In this chapter, we look at medical-information companies and other healthcare organizations that are making the most of their customer assets, which include relationships with customers, channels, and affiliates. Our goal is to demonstrate how healthcare organizations can create value with their customers. (In the case of medical-information providers, the customers are the people who sign on to access the data services.)

AOL has more than 27 million of them, which, with its market value of more than $150 billion (prior to its merger with Time Warner), means that the value generated per customer is approximately $1,000. Another case in point is the recent purchase by China Mobile, Ltd., the largest operator of cell phones in the Peoples Republic of China, of almost 24 million customers for $35 billion from China Telecom, Ltd., its affiliated parent. It is clear that no matter how customer relationships are reported, no successful business

> "As a CEO, there's nothing that humbles you quicker and more effectively than dealing with the customer. Your own people might tell you that you're brilliant, but your customers will tell you how it is."
>
> — R. David Yost,
> *president and chief executive officer,*
> *AmeriSource Health Corporation.*

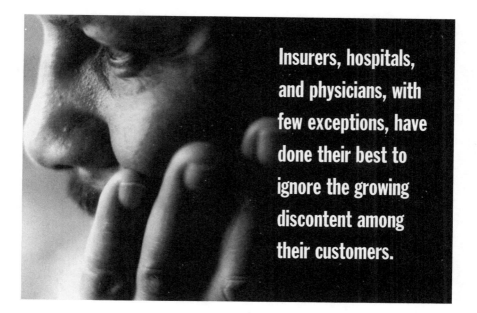

Insurers, hospitals, and physicians, with few exceptions, have done their best to ignore the growing discontent among their customers.

leader underestimates their importance.

How does your healthcare company identify, manage, and determine how much to invest in its relationships with customers? In fact, does your enterprise know how many customers it has or how often and what they purchase from you? Does it know their value?

Chances are, you haven't organized customer-loyalty programs either, even though they have become commonplace in other industries. MCI WorldCom, Inc., for example, has "friends and family." AOL has "buddies." All the airlines have frequent-flier plans. They are useful strategies designed to win customers' loyalty.

To be sure, relationships with customers, are neither measured nor managed in the same way as financial or physical assets. But that need not interfere with your constructing a business model around them. Common sense and an understanding of what matters will show you that customers and other intangible assets are at the core of today's most valuable business models.

In most industries, the borders that separate product and service providers from consumers have been blurred, if not obliterated altogether. In healthcare, most of the barriers remain. Insurers, hospitals, and physicians, with few exceptions, have managed to ignore the growing discontent among their customers.

Customers.

Fortunately, that has not stopped customers from asking questions or outside companies from answering them. Now, parents worried about their children's health, adult children concerned about their aging parents, or ill people undergoing confusing treatments have new places, online resources, where they can find answers — away from a doctor's examining room, a hospital admissions office, and without visiting an emergency room.

Forty percent of Americans report that television is their primary and often preferred source for health news and information. Online organizations, such as AOL, and a bevy of health-related Web sites are battling to create a subscription base to attract advertisers. Customers seem to be ready for new sources of substantive information on health and illness.

As we mentioned in the previous chapter, one name that is gaining considerable attention — and building substantial and valuable customer relationships — is WebMD Corporation, based in Atlanta, Georgia.

Who: WebMD Corporation.
How: It aggregates customers.

WebMD has an audacious goal: It seeks to make the Internet the common, shared base for all healthcare information. Its plan is to enlist employers, doctors, health-maintenance organizations, and hospitals as paying subscribers who will provide services that eventually will allow everyone to conduct his or her healthcare business over the Web.

This would mean that you could sign up for healthcare coverage, choose your doctor, obtain a referral to a specialist, schedule an appointment, discuss your claim with your HMO, and request copies of your medical records by accessing a single Web site. Insurers could electronically disburse funds and approve referrals. Healthcare providers and insurance carriers would be able to send information to customers who, in turn, could ask questions of plan administrators.

Furthermore, such a system would facilitate portable healthcare, which, right now is a goal the federal government, the single biggest contributor of healthcare money, is strenuously promoting. As of now, a visitor to WebMD is limited to browsing in a substantial body of healthcare information. But the company has taken steps toward realizing its larger goals with its purchase of OnHealth.com, a well-subscribed health site. That gives WebMD a total of 10 million visitors, making it the largest health site to date.

WebMD's connections to doctors and hospitals are yet to be realized. But those providers have good reasons to join. Doctors, for example, could submit insurance claims and patient bills online; they could also speed prescriptions to pharmacists.

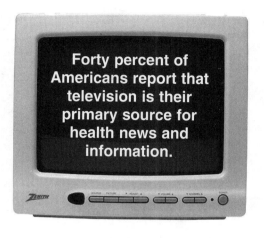

Forty percent of Americans report that television is their primary source for health news and information.

WebMD has created a huge customer base, from which it can move on to its next stage. It is creating value with its customers.

Recognition of the crucial value of a reliable and supportive customer-asset base is not unique to e-business, software, or information companies. Businesses in every industry must have such a base, or they will fail in our global economy. The customers everyone is trying to sell to may number in the millions, but they are not infinite.

> "... the one success factor
> that I consider absolutely critical:
> an organization's ability
> to attract valuable customers,
> both now and in the future.
> This is vital because today's most serious
> business challenge doesn't involve implementing
> new management techniques, raising capital,
> or any of the familiar bugaboos
> of recent decades.
> Today's most serious business challenge
> is a scarcity of customers."
>
> — Fred Wiersema, *The New Market Leaders.*

To create its own niche in the midst of this contest, UnitedHealth Group, Inc., based in Minnetonka, Minnesota, distinguished itself from virtually every other company in its industry.

Who: UnitedHealth Group, Inc.
How: It offers choice to its customers to promote loyalty and repeat purchases.

In the fall of 1999, UnitedHealth Group, along with every other HMO in the United States, was feeling the heat of accumulated criticism from patients, physicians, and Congress. The latest blow: Legislation that would give patients the right to sue managed-care companies for malpractice was being considered by a Senate-House conference committee in Washington, D.C.

At the center of the controversy was the long-time policy that required doctors to receive permission from their patients' HMOs before either hospitalizing them or referring them for more specialized treatment. In November, United, the second-largest health insurer in the nation, took the unprecedented step of eliminating that caveat from its policies, returning to doctors the right to recommend treatments for their patients.

A number of reasons contributed to United's decision, but none was more important than the company's concern for its 14.5 million customers. By easing their access to care, the company was increasing the likelihood of retaining its customers and substantially improving its chances of attracting new ones.

With this decision, the company earned respect from the nation's physicians and set itself apart from its competitors. "It's always a good idea when the patient and doctor decide what's best for the patient, so we welcome this decision," Dr. Bruce Malone, a veteran orthopedic surgeon, recently said. "We had a lot of ridiculous requirements that we call and get approval for every session, every X-ray. It only makes sense that they stop it."

United's leaders said that the old policy was no longer needed as a means to control costs. "Consumers and physicians are much more intelligent about the economics of healthcare," noted Rick Cook, a United executive. "They are much more sensitive to cost issues than they were 10 years ago." In addition to winning the approval of patients and doctors, this move saved United the $100-million-a-year cost of processing referral and procedure requests.

"UnitedHealth Group has consistently sought ways

to provide tangible value to its customers —

whether individual consumers, businesses,

governments, or other healthcare institutions.

In that pursuit, our view of value

in the marketplace has included

not just the measurement of the price

of services, but also their convenience,

quality, and consistency

with the underlying values of the customer."

— William W. McGuire, M.D., *chairman and chief executive officer, United Health Group, Inc.*

United continues to monitor member physicians to weed out those who consistently fail to meet the HMO's guidelines. But even in those cases, it no longer imposes itself between doctors and patients in real time.

Also influencing United's policy change was the legislative climate in the nation's capitol, and, indeed, throughout the country. Class-action lawsuits had already been filed blaming HMOs, not physicians, for bad medical results. Ultimately, the wisdom of the company's decision to remove itself from the middle of the patient-doctor relationship was evidenced by the loyalty of its existing customers and a substantial increase in new ones. United has undoubtedly demonstrated its ability to create value with its customers.

Amgen, Inc., the world's largest biotechnology concern which we discussed in Chapter 5 in the context of financial assets, has a different, but equally effective approach to customers.

Who: Amgen, Inc.
How: It supports and keeps its customers with free programs.

The 20-year-old Amgen develops and manufactures drugs that treat a variety of ailments, including auto-immune and blood-cell diseases. One of its most promising products, Infergen, is used for the treatment of hepatitis C virus (HCV). An estimated 4 million Americans suffer from the effects of HCV, which can lead to liver failure, cirrhosis of the liver, and cancer, and the number is increasing sharply. Many were infected through blood transfusions received prior to 1990, when effective blood screening first became routine. Others were intravenous drug users who contracted the virus by sharing needles.

Amgen's actual and potential Infergen customers include the patients themselves, of course, but also the medical professionals and caregivers who dispense medications. The company has created two programs to establish and strengthen its relationships with them.

The first program features a comprehensive manual, *How to Start a Hepatitis C Support Group*, which includes advice on finding local experts, recruiting members, and raising funds. Research has shown that members of support groups are more likely to master self-care techniques and to rate the quality of their lives higher than do other HCV patients. The group members report less anxiety and depression, and studies indicate that patients who are more informed about and involved in their care actually live longer.

In addition to the free manual, Amgen established a telephone support line called Compass, which is staffed around the clock by healthcare professionals who provide callers with reliable information about the virus, Infergen treatment, and further resources, such as the American Liver Foundation. Compass also connects HCV patients in financial need with the company's Safety Net program, which is designed to assure that Amgen's medications are not denied to appropriate candidates for financial reasons. Favorably impressed with the company's initiatives, patients and providers alike are developing stronger relationships with Amgen.

As a biotechnology company, Amgen sells ideas. It thus invests primarily in proprietary knowledge, an organization asset in Value-Dynamics terms. But that does not hinder the company from successfully making the most of its customers as well.

Having a savvy strategy that uses its entire portfolio of assets and relationships to create value is a trademark of a successful organization in today's economy — Amgen is surely that.

Channels.

We include channels in our customer category, because they facilitate the transfer of goods or services from an enterprise to all of its customers. When a representative of a surgical-supply company informs your surgeon that a brand new part is available for your knee replacement, that representative is a channel for the new product. Thus, relationships with channel partners, such as distributors, marketing agents, and advertising agencies, are necessary to your company's go-to-market model and, as such, must be considered sources of value in your business model.

"... it's not management who decides how many people are on the payroll, **it's customers.**"

— Lawrence A. Bossidy, *retired chairman, Honeywell, Inc.*

Channels are to business what your arteries are to your heart . Like a business with unstable conduits or channels, the person with a blocked or torn artery is not long for this world. Channel companies that actually take title to a product before selling it to someone else are called merchant middlemen; drug wholesalers and retailers fall into this category. Today, online channels open the door to audiences and markets of previously unimagined breadth and depth.

Who: AmeriSource Health Corporation, Bergen Brunswig Drug Company, Cardinal Health, Inc., and McKesson HBOC, Inc.

How: They build powerful channels.

These companies, our nation's four largest pharmaceutical wholesalers, are bullish about their prospects, and for good reason. They are the leaders in a market that is projected to grow 10 to 11 percent annually for at least the next 2 years.

R. David Yost, president and chief executive officer of AmeriSource Health Corporation, of Malvern, Pennsylvania, attributes this optimism to a unique combination of occurrences. Topping the list is the fact that baby boomers are aging. With 85 million people poised to pass the half-century mark by 2005, wholesalers are at the epicenter of a healthcare explosion. A greater demand for expensive drugs will combine with general price inflation to make the boom even more explosive.

When asked if managed care will inhibit the lucrative market for drug distribution, Yost explained that he expects just the opposite to occur. "Pharmaceutical therapy is part of the solution to arresting the nation's healthcare costs," he said, explaining that it is less expensive than the alternatives of more care by doctors or no care at all.

Another positive factor for many pharmaceuticals, according to David Neu, head of marketing at Orange, California's Bergen Brunswig Drug Company, is the large number of drug patents that are scheduled to expire over the next few years. The burst of generic and over-the-counter substitutes that is sure to follow will consume a major share of the pharmaceutical portion of the healthcare pie.

Moreover, some surgical procedures are being supplanted by drug therapies. Mark Majeske, whose company, McKesson HBOC, Inc., has its headquarters in San Francisco, California, pointed out that research-and-development spending has resulted in a new generation of aggressive drugs to treat illnesses that once required surgery. Medicines such as Tagamet and Zantac used for stomach ailments are examples.

In addition to deriving additional revenues from scientific, demographic, and price changes, pharmaceutical companies are increasing their sales and profits by offering added value to their retailer customers. These pharmacies — channels, in Value Dynamics lexicon — can benefit from an array of new programs and services designed to promote their efficiency and effectiveness.

Cardinal Health, Inc., in Dublin, Ohio, knows that one way pharmacies build consumer equity, particularly with chronic patients, is by providing immediate access to new prescription products. To aid in that goal, it has designed a rapid distribution program that gets new drugs onto pharmacy shelves within 48 hours of their approval by the U.S. Food and Drug Administration.

Cardinal has also ridden its channel expertise into whole new profit areas. Cardinal managers, said Lawrence C. Marsh, senior vice president of the equity research department of Lehman Brothers, "have done a very good job over the years of applying their core competency in the distribution business . . . to other pharmacy-services businesses. They are in areas such as hospital-pharmacy management, automated dispensing technology . . . and they are even in the packaging of pharmaceuticals in drug delivery."

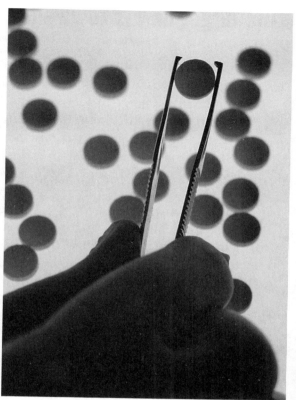

"We see the pharmacist of the future being totally involved in customers' healthcare management, and being paid for it."

—R. David Yost, *president and chief executive officer, AmeriSource Corporation.*

In anticipation of an expanding role for the retail pharmacist, channel suppliers, such as AmeriSource Health, are working to provide new support systems. "We see the pharmacist of the future being totally involved in customers' healthcare management, and being paid for it," CEO Yost said.

AmeriSource Health has developed a program on managing disease that is intended to educate pharmacists in monitoring their customers'

"The target now is to invent a new game."

— Philip N. Knight, *founder, chairman, chief executive officer, and president, Nike, Inc.*

drug regimens. With this training, pharmacists are better prepared to help consumers comply with their sometimes very complex regimens. Included in the program, too, is training that the pharmacists are encouraged to share with customers, such as information for diabetics whose lives depend upon an unwavering adherence to a drug-and-diet plan.

McKesson, which secured an exclusive long-term supply agreement with Rite Aid Corporation in 1998, adds value to that affiliation by providing its channel customer with expertise in inventory management and technological resources, as well as delivering its product. McKesson's InfoLink technology gives Rite Aid real-time analyses of product usage and inventory information at the store level. It also has dedicated a customer-service team, specifically trained in Rite Aid procedures, to respond quickly to individual store needs.

At Bergen Brunswig, David Neu identifies home healthcare as "probably the fastest-growing healthcare sector today." His company offers pharmacies a complete line of durable home-healthcare equipment, such as wheelchairs, beds, and bath accessories, along with assistance in creating the right product mix and store layout.

Bergen consultants offer professional manuals, training aids, and continuing education programs to employees at the retail level. To help pharmacies gain reimbursement from government and private insurers for cognitive services, the company has designed a patient-interview technique.

Such value-added initiatives are leading wholesalers well beyond cost-effective drug distribution and into the realms of education, marketing, and technology. Having recognized that they expand their markets by strengthening their retailer customers, the drug wholesalers are now making the most of their channels as a way of creating value for their own shareholders.

Affiliates.

Along with channel relationships, we include affiliates in the customer category. Although in accounting parlance, the designation "affiliate" implies specific stock-ownership guidelines, we are defining it in looser, relational terms — that is, as closely associated organizations. In the language of Value Dynamics, these inter-organizational relationships facilitate the marketing and sales of products and services. They are an example of networking and connectivity.

Who: PSIHealth.net, Inc.
How: It invests in affiliates.

PSIHealth.net, Inc., based in Wilmington, Massachusetts, provides computer-system technology and support to healthcare professionals. PSI thinks of Sickbay.com as its affiliate in its effort "to develop and communicate a cost-effective approach to healthcare."

Sickbay is an online provider of healthcare information and discounted products and services and refers to itself as "the fastest-growing healthcare portal on the Internet." Members can access its online billing and appointment-scheduling service. They also can meet online professionals who use its support services in a secure environment.

It is likely that this sort of mutually beneficial affiliation will become more prototypical.

▶ What's Next?

The organization assets of any company — its systems, processes, culture, mission, leadership, brands, and proprietary knowledge — could easily be described as its central nervous system. Because of the humane, often humanitarian, nature of the healthcare business, the analogy seems especially appropriate, and terms such as culture, mission, and leadership have a particular resonance.

In the next chapter, we examine, one by one, these intangible assets that in many ways give meaning to the work we do in the healthcare industry.

Questions to ask yourself.

Business Model: Is your healthcare organization effectively creating, managing, and investing in its relationships with its customers to create value? Focus on customers, channels, and affiliates and ask yourself whether your company knows all it needs to regarding how to make these relationships endure. If you consider customers as nothing more than a source of revenue, you are not creating the value you could.

Risk: How do your organization's relationships with customers work within its business model to create value? Does it have non-paying customers, as AOL does, or is it only comfortable with conventional paying customers? Furthermore, do its customer risk-management systems have a way of assessing the cost of losing as well as acquiring customers?

Technology: Can you extrapolate ideas from the case studies featured in this chapter that will help you manage your customer relationships more effectively? Has your company installed customer relationship-management systems? Does it offer loyalty programs to win greater allegiance to your enterprise? Do you have a customer-information system that allows consumers to reserve any product or service you sell or could make available through your network of suppliers?

Measurement: What methods does your healthcare organization use to track and measure the value-creating contributions of its customers? Its channels? Its affiliates? Does it measure the cost of acquisitions on an individual basis? Can it calculate the discounted cash flow from that acquisition over the course of the relationship? Is your company familiar with the specific nature of its relationship with a customer, by which we mean: What is its duration; what, how much, and how often does that customer purchase? Finally, does it know the market value of its entire customer base? A portion of it? If the answer to any of these questions is, "I don't know," then your company is vulnerable to the loss of some of its most precious sources of value.

8 WHO'S CREATING VALUE WITH ORGANIZATION ASSETS?

A strategy and its enactment are central to the success or failure of a company and cannot be overlooked when determining that company's worth.

In the fall of 1996, William W. George, chief executive officer of Medtronic, Inc., the medical device manufacturer, sent an e-mail message to all of his company's 20,000 employees.

His wife was recovering from breast cancer, and George wanted to report on her condition. His words reflected his deep capacity to draw lessons from personal experience.

He wrote, in part: "This experience has transformed both of us in many ways. It has helped us to live more in the moment, to know ultimately we have nothing to fear, and to recognize at a deeper level that healing is not just about surgery, but depends upon . . . the whole person — body, mind, heart, and spirit."

We will return to discuss George and Medtronic shortly; for now, we will simply point out that his ability to inspire his employees is paired with an impressive talent for making and carrying out tough decisions. He epitomizes leadership, one of the organization assets that are the focus of this chapter.

Organization assets, as defined by Value Dynamics, function as the nervous system of your enterprise. They link all of the other assets and relationships into a collective whole, building the business model that will ultimately determine your company's value-creating capabilities now and well into the future.

In addition to leadership, the Value Dynamics Framework includes the following categories under the rubric of organization assets: strategy, structure, processes, systems, culture and values, brands, and proprietary knowledge. We will offer examples of many of these assets in the pages ahead.

Too often, organization assets are not recognized as potential creators of value, because they are perceived as too intangible. That perception is greatly flawed. These assets actually provide the glue that holds an enterprise together. Since, in our view, the most intangible assets are the most enduring and valuable, organization assets may be a company's most important. For example, it is hard to imagine what remains of a pharmaceutical company if it loses its patents, or what is left of a hospital if its culture and values disappear. Doctors' offices would become chaotic without systems, and insurance companies could not survive if they failed to establish and maintain their brands.

Organization assets must be invested in, managed, and measured wisely. But the first step is to make sure they are identified and recognized as assets. Otherwise, companies cannot begin to become value creators.

Organizational assets enable one asset to work with another, one network to talk to another, and one decision to mesh with another. They are the cornerstones of change and value creation in this century. Developing new ways to maximize the value of these assets may lead your organization to examine its very foundation. That kind of insight can transform a company. Leaders, such as Henry J. Kaiser, a pioneer in both healthcare and manufacturing, have that insight. Once, when he was asked how he looked at business difficulties, he responded, "Problems are only opportunities in work clothes."

Leadership.

One company that has a deep understanding of the value of leadership is Medtronic.

Who: Medtronic, Inc.
How: William George leads the way.

When William George became chief executive of Medtronic in 1991, the $1-billion company was still the industry leader in the manufacture of heart pacemakers (an implanted device that accelerates a slow heartbeat) and defibrillators (used to slow down a rapid heartbeat). Anticipating growing competition within his industry and concerned that his company's future was less certain than it had been, George immediately confronted the question of how Medtronic could enhance its product lines.

He could have concentrated on acquisitions, indulged in a technological buying spree, or purchased the rights to others' innovations — all aimed at developing the company's expertise in new areas. Instead, George decided that the company's future should be built upon its two basic technologies: implantation and stimulation. They would have to be leveraged to develop and market new product lines.

As we saw in Chapter 2, George knew that the 8 percent of receipts the company dedicated to research and development had to increase. He seized upon a windfall from the settlement of patent-infringement suits to push research and development up to 11 percent of receipts, where it has remained ever since. The results have been gratifying. Medtronic has developed a range of new products, including cardiac-surgery equipment, heart valves, catheters for angioplasty, and devices for treating pain.

Part of the success can be attributed to George's introduction of small, specialized teams at headquarters and at the divisional level. Focusing on everything from new product ideas to marketing, they function, as George puts it, "off-line, out of the mainstream organizations." For the most part, team members are front-line people who think creatively against the norm, then enact their ideas. George's dedication to the team concept extends to senior managers as well. "All executive members participate in every major decision," he recently said.

George often takes hiking trips to sites where he cannot be reached by his office, but he doesn't worry: "It's not like I'm leaving the company alone. I'm not a one-person band around here."

As a leader, George treasures independent thinking in his employees. His Quest Program awards $50,000 per person to 6 to 8 Medtronic employees each year. Recipients use the awards to pursue projects that

Good leaders possess the capacity to communicate, the willingness to do so, and a genuine pleasure in the interactions.

fall outside of their customary zones of operations. He makes it clear that he wants employees to take appropriate risks and will protect those who do so. Mike James, vice president of marketing for the company's pacemaker business, has explained that "many examples of risk taking [are] rewarded, and failures [do] not end with beheadings."

George initiated a system in which five generations of a product are maintained simultaneously, from concept to launch, which has cut by more than a third, the time it takes to commercialize a product. "Stacking products like that has given us a tremendous competitive edge," he noted. "Now we don't just come up with one product and watch the competition try to come out with something better." More than a third of the company's sales are derived from products launched in the past year.

In addition to his uncanny abilities to make excellent choices and devise appropriate policies and systems to realize them, George possesses another attribute essential for a good leader — the capacity to communicate, the willingness to do so, and a genuine pleasure in the interactions.

He constantly uses e-mail to encourage or challenge individuals as well as to make company-wide broadcasts. He sees his e-mail messages as a way to get Medtronic's people "up and down the organization, in the same direction, and in concert." He exemplifies what good leaders do and how crucial they are to the overall success of today's business models.

> "A leader is not appointed because he knows everything and can make every decision. He is appointed to bring together the knowledge that is available, and then create the prerequisites for the work to be done. He creates the systems that enable him to delegate responsibility for day-to-day operations."
>
> — Jan Carlzon, *former chairman and chief executive officer, Scandinavian Airlines System.*

Strategy.

A leader who lacks well-articulated strategies is of no use (and can bring harm) to a business. In business, as in war, a strategy is a crucial asset — the blueprint for action that will win or lose not only a battle or two, but the entire campaign.

The army that has the best plan for maximizing and deploying its troops and weaponry, its military assets, is going to win, assuming its forces are comparable in strength to those of its enemy.

The corporation with a strategy that makes the most of its assets and unrealized opportunities in its marketplace is also going to win. Of course, in the corporate world, according to Value Dynamics, the truly effective strategy in today's economy must be based on the full range of a company's assets with particular attention paid to the intangibles. Among those intangible assets is the company's strategy. The strategy and its enactment are central to the success or failure of a company and cannot be overlooked when determining that company's worth.

A company that has successfully integrated the value of strategy into its business model is Cerner Corporation.

Who: Cerner Corporation.
How: Its strategy is to facilitate the flow of information.

When three information-systems experts formed Cerner in 1979, their strategy called for developing systems that would automate the flow of data in an industry where such technology was rarely, if ever, used. Their target industry turned out to be healthcare.

It took the company five years to bring out its first product, which was called PathNet and was designed as an information system for medical laboratories. When PathNet was accepted by the labs, Cerner started building similar systems for radiology, pulmonary medicine, and respiratory care.

Each system was constructed on the same foundation, which meant that, eventually, the various sites would be able to share information easily. Many customers were attracted by the fact that Cerner's systems focused on the exchange of information about specific patients, as well as on financial data, because it fit well with the growing trend toward managed care. In fact, the company's strategy of developing systems that could blend the information that flowed between the medical and the business facets of a healthcare organization met an important need in the early 1990s.

But, by the late 1990s, Cerner had a new strategy in place. The company was determined to become the nation's leader in the design of healthcare information systems for the Internet. With its IQHealth division, conceived specifically to achieve that goal, the company once again demonstrated its ability to create new value with its strategy assets.

Cerner had a new strategy in place. It was determined to become the nation's leader in the design of healthcare information systems for the Internet.

In addition to healthcare companies, the target customers included any organization that provided health programs for its employees. Cerner's software makes it possible for patients to be in private, online contact with physicians and health systems, sharing information that can identify and resolve an employee's illness.

Some of IQHealth's special services are impressive. For example, the system allows patients to construct a complete record of their family's healthcare for their own and their physicians' reference. The service includes surveys that assess patients' health, information about follow-up and preventive care programs, and a guide to help assure the proper use of both over-the-counter and prescribed medications.

IQHealth provides services that attract and retain customers, and does so while saving valuable time and money for those customers as well as for physicians and other healthcare providers and organizations. Using the Internet or an intranet to link caregivers with patients and with each other, Cerner improves the speed and accuracy of their communication and reduces expenses by making information instantly accessible.

> "During the 1990s, several core strategies defined
> our company. Over the next 10 years,
> these strategies will continue to define
> Cerner, and, we believe, our industry.
> In an environment that is constantly changing,
> with enormous opportunities emerging
> from within as well as from without,
> we believe the consistency
> of these core strategies creates
> tremendous strength, stability, and leverage
> for Cerner today and well into the new millennium."
>
> — Neal L. Patterson, *chairman and chief executive officer, Cerner Corporation.*

Structure.

A well-reasoned strategy cannot be executed successfully without an equally well-constructed organizational structure.

The urge to comprehend organizational structure can be traced as far back as the Middle Ages when European churches used diagrams that presented an outline of their hierarchy. These outlines, which the French call *organigramme*, remain a convenient tool for visualizing the chain of command and its interstices for any company, be it an insurance carrier or a hospital.

To understand in detail how an enterprise fits together requires closer study. The neat lines of an organization chart reveal only what is intended, not the reality of relationships. Many supervisors, for example, are held hostage by their supervisees, while many chief executives have yielded control to their executive committees.

Since, to an important degree, the structure of an organization determines how efficiently it operates, the Value Dynamics Framework treats structure as a separate asset. As such, it needs to be carefully analyzed and understood to realize its full potential. The corporate structure of 100-year-old Johnson & Johnson (J&J) is world famous for its achievements.

Who: Johnson & Johnson.
How: Its structure fosters agility.

The $27-billion-a-year pharmaceutical giant employs nearly 98,000 people in more than 190 distinct operating enterprises in 51 countries around the world.

In the early 1990s, J&J became concerned over a business environment that was becoming more competitive and less defined, and worried that its enormous size would make it vulnerable to complacency. As a result, the company undertook a structural reorganization that would enable it to be more nimble and responsive to change.

The scattered and largely independent fiefdoms that had always characterized J&J were given new marching orders. Rather than focusing so much on the results of their individual operations, the managers of the individual divisions were told to integrate the corporate perspective into their individual strategies and decisions. They were provided with a more thorough grounding in precisely what circumstances and problems the company as a whole was confronting. The message: J&J is one company.

The company's leaders arrived at a dramatic and innovative approach that would somewhat alter its traditional corporate structure. They designed a program and named it FrameworkS, which was intentionally written with a capital S at the end to signify and reinforce the idea that there are many "frames," through which everyone needs to look at their various businesses — particularly, the larger corporate frame. Under FrameworkS, the decentralized structure remained in place, but managers and employees in the individual divisions were brought into direct contact with corporate management, and the executive committee was given a greater voice in the operations of the divisions.

In its first stage, FrameworkS gathered 700 of the company's sharpest minds in marketing, science, technology, and management from around the world. They met with senior corporate managers at headquarters to discuss policy and consider strategies that would affect the entire organization.

Then the executive committee named a series of FrameworkS teams, each of which was given a specific project; task forces from those teams were assigned to research and investigate particular topics that, for the most part, had little to do directly with their home division.

FrameworkS research is arduous, taking into account analyses of operating procedures, as well as overall policies and specific practices. Any given project will take about six months and require substantial time and energy from team managers who also have to perform their regular, often demanding assignments. For instance, one team was sent to Japan to see if the company's position in that market could be strengthened, and came back with about 1,000 possible courses of action.

When completed, the results of an investigation are evaluated and analyzed at a full meeting of a FrameworkS team and the executive committee. The meetings' goal is not to resolve specific problems, although that happens, but to foster free-flowing discussions where assumptions are discarded and preconceived ideas are challenged. Once decisions are made, management teams draw up plans that lead to action programs, in which the ideas are realized.

As of this writing, 10 FrameworkS have been conducted, resulting in some unexpected initiatives. The company has entered new markets, founded new businesses, and established programs in technology and recruitment. Innovation is encouraged and new leadership candidates have emerged.

Ralph J. Larsen, Johnson & Johnson's chairman and chief executive officer, believes that FrameworkS has succeeded in "releasing energy throughout the corporation, and focusing the eyes of the organization and its leadership on the two most important issues [in] our future — innovation and growth."

"Because we are decentralized and have 190 operating companies around the world, we have the benefits of being big with the benefits of being small. So our decentralized operating companies are nimble. They're quick. The largest of our companies is only about $2 billion."

— Ralph J. Larsen
chairman and chief executive officer,
Johnson & Johnson.

The program has also led to a subtle structural change. Management now plays a larger role in the initiatives of various divisions without compromising the decentralized status and independence of those units. It has been an impressive example of a company's ability to make the most of its structure assets to create new value for the organization.

Processes.

Processes, another crucial organization asset, are what enable a company to execute its strategy. From the reengineering movement, we learned that all processes, especially those closest to customers, are valuable assets to any business. Without them, there would be no conduit through which your organization's strategies can be realized.

When James Champy and Michael Hammer introduced the concept of reengineering, they defined a process as a series of tasks, including operations, actions, and functions, that together create a product or service. They told us that every company must identify, map, and measure its processes if it wants to exploit them to provide new value for its stakeholders.

Who: Pfizer, Inc.
How: Its rapid drug commercialization process.

Pharmaceutical maker Pfizer boasts perhaps the richest new-product pipeline in the drug business, with 16 medications in advanced development or registration and some 55 compounds in early development — among them, drugs to treat cancer, depression, diabetes, obesity, and stroke.

On average, it takes pharmaceutical companies 190 person-years to move a compound through the various stages of development from discovery to clinical trials. In the industry overall, just one out of every 7 million compounds that undergo screening actually reach drugstore shelves.

At Pfizer, the process takes less than a third of the average time. In its determination to keep its product pipeline full, the company is constantly elaborating and improving upon the intense, focused series of steps that move ideas toward their ultimate fate, as either marketable products or also-rans.

With dozens of compounds in the testing process at any particular time, one major challenge is to discard, as early as possible, those that are not going to become commercial products. But, as in most areas of research, scientists who spend years working on a project often develop an emotional commitment to it and will battle to keep it alive.

Pfizer addresses this problem with a strategy that extracts data from its drug-testing process, and, in addition, paves the way to increased value. A "step chart," which is set up for each potential drug, indicates the number of promising compounds that should be in place at each stage. The charts help everyone involved in a project see how it is progressing at different stages and what remains to be done.

The payoff for this turbo-charged process is a stable of strong-selling drugs.

Systems.

In the Value Dynamics Framework, as in the world at large, asset categories are dependent upon each other. Of what value would processes be, for example, without the physical and electronic systems available in today's wired world? In a sense, the systems in companies resemble those in our bodies. In both cases, there must be input to produce output, and certainly, in both cases, they are absolutely essential to the survival of the organism.

Wireless and wireline, front- and back-office, transaction and analytical are just some of the systems assets at a company's disposal. Interacting with each other, these systems, which require a panoply of equipment, technology, and software, assure that enormously complex business organisms run smoothly and efficiently. Also included in our definition are codified knowledge-management systems that assemble, organize, and direct the flow of information to those who need it.

Who: The Kaiser Foundation Health Plan, Inc.
How: It built a clinical-information network.

The Kaiser Foundation Health Plan, Inc., is a company that understands the value of systems and is well aware of the investment required to make them work at their peak. Witness its investment of $1 billion to transform its computerized clinical-information system into a national network. The move was a first for the industry, but that was no surprise. Since Henry J.

Kaiser established the company in 1945 as the first public program for low-cost, prepaid medical care, his programs have been pioneers.

Kaiser, a high school dropout, won fame as a builder, first of government dams during the Depression, and then of the 1,400 Liberty cargo ships that played an important role in World War II. His Kaiser Permanente Health Plan, the first true health maintenance organization, grew out of a health insurance program that he structured for his shipyard workers during the war and his construction workers before that. It was condemned by the medical establishment as socialized medicine. In fact, many states outlawed HMOs at the time, but Kaiser remained undaunted and his organization grew enormously.

"Technology is everybody's business."

— Donald L. Boudreau, Chase Manhattan Corporation.

Today, Kaiser, based in Oakland, California, is the largest health-insurance non-profit in the country, covering more than 8 million members in 17 states and is rapidly growing.

Its state-of-the-art electronic information system is designed to allow the company to compete more effectively by delivering unmatched quality healthcare. The information system will connect Kaiser Permanente's 10,000 physicians, as well as nurses and other treatment providers, with each other. In addition, they will all have access to the 9 million patient records stored in a standard digital format.

Instead of the inevitable delays, confusions and errors that occur when patient information is maintained on paper, the new system will enable physicians and nurses to access data immediately, accelerating both diagnosis and treatment.

A patient's medical chart is nothing more than a bundle of papers upon which a doctor has documented information regarding a patient's symptoms, diseases, surgeries, medications, and allergies. It could take hours to find and decipher a specific piece of information in a particular patient's chart, which, of course, is unacceptable in an emergency. If the original doctor is unavailable, parts of the record may be totally inaccessible. Instead, when the record is maintained in digital form, it becomes an invaluable resource for any doctor or nurse.

The new network offers other benefits as well, which can be previewed at Kaiser's regional centers, where the individual systems have been upgraded with an additional $500 million worth of equipment. At the Portland, Oregon, center, for example, when a physician types in a prescription for Zoloft, an antidepressant, she triggers a note on her computer screen pointing out that Zoloft is far more expensive than some other drugs that perform in a similar way. When a patient needs to refill his prescriptions, he phones his request to his doctor, who enters it into the system, which automatically dispatches it to the Kaiser pharmacy. The refill is mailed to the patient within two days.

Physicians in the Portland system can also order lab tests and request referrals on their computers. They have access to Medline, the national database of medical journal abstracts, and they can search 28 medical textbooks online for specific information. They are reminded when their patients are due for particular lab tests or X-rays, and they are alerted if a Kaiser member has been treated at an emergency room.

To help gain the enthusiastic cooperation of its physicians, who work exclusively for the Kaiser Permanente Medical Care Program, in the shift from paper to digital operations, the company has encouraged them to participate in the development of the new system. Thus, what had been Kaiser's cost disadvantage in relation to competitors — its huge bank of in-house, highly paid professionals — has been converted into a major advantage because of the leveraging of its technology.

Kaiser identified the limitations of its information system and allocated the funds to transform it into a state-of-the-art national information network. Now, it is truly positioned to make the most of its system assets.

Culture and Values.

Among all the organizations' assets, the two that are perhaps least appreciated by most company leaders today are values and culture. It may be currently fashionable for managers to talk to their employees and to the public about values, but that doesn't mean that later they won't be ignored, especially in difficult times. In the words of William F. Buckley, Jr.: "Idealism is fine, but, as it approaches reality, the cost becomes prohibitive."

In the Value Dynamics Framework, the culture and values of an organization, written and unwritten, are recognized as assets that have to be taken very seriously. One major reason: They guide employees toward making good decisions without consulting supervisors, a scenario that is at the heart of efficient operations in leading-edge companies today.

Values express the standards of behavior that are so vital to success in today's economy. Furthermore, because culture and values assets are capable of being leveraged, they can increase the overall worth of the organization.

Let's look at LensCrafters, Inc. as an example of a company that demonstrates its appreciation for and knowledge of how to use its culture and values to their full potential.

Who: LensCrafters, Inc.
How: It has far-sighted values.

If you wear glasses, you know what a complicated affair it can be getting new ones. You have to visit an optometrist, have your eyes tested, receive a prescription that you take to an optician, and then wait for a week or two to get your new glasses. It is a time-consuming and expensive process, and, until 1983, there was no alternative.

That was when LensCrafters opened its first store, applying retailing techniques to the world of eyeglasses. Set up in convenient locations, the stores were open nights and weekends equipped and staffed to craft custom-made lenses on the spot. And next to each store, the company leased space and equipment to a licensed optometrist. Customers were guaranteed a pair of glasses in approximately one hour, once the optometrist's prescription was dropped off at the store.

LensCrafters, acquired by Italy's Luxottica Group S.p.A. in 1995, made 4 more promises to its customers: a 30-day no-risk guarantee; a price-match guarantee; a free lifetime maintenance guarantee; and a one-year protection plan if the glasses were to break.

Yet, despite the benefits it offered, the company still faced an uphill struggle, because of the longtime trust and loyalty that people felt for their eye doctors and opticians. That LensCrafters was able to climb that hill to its current success is owed, in part, to the values built into the organization at an early stage and constantly leveraged over the years since.

According to David Browne, the former president of LensCrafters, the company "recognizes that helping people is a greater calling than selling eyeglasses." That value is reflected in the quick and efficient service customers receive, but it is also expressed in a program called Give the Gift of Sight, which offers a variety of activities related to vision care. The program is sponsored by the company and its foundation, in partnership with local and national charities.

Since its inception in 1988, Give the Gift of Sight has helped nearly

2 million needy children and adults in North America and around the world. Two 40-foot Vision Vans, named Seemore and Iris, travel coast to coast through inner cities, Indian reservations, and rural areas to deliver free eye care to children. The vans are equipped and staffed by LensCrafters' volunteers and affiliated doctors. They have distributed more than 3 million pairs of contributed glasses to needy people, and doctors allied with the company have provided eye care, free of charge, to more than 250,000 people. Give the Gift of Sight and other humanitarian projects give LensCrafters employees and allied optometrists a sense of pride and value in their organization. They also work to attract and retain loyal customers. That's a lot of value to get from your values.

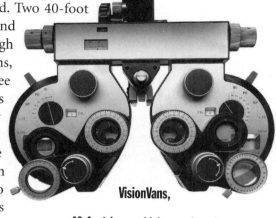

VisionVans, 40-foot-long vehicles equipped and staffed by LensCrafters, deliver free eye care to the poor, to disaster areas, and to remote parts of the United States.

Brands.

By many measures and according to several experts, the one asset that may be most valuable in this century is your brand. Nothing signifies more clearly to your investors, suppliers, employees, and customers what you stand for and how you will create value than your brand.

A brand may be a name, sign, or symbol attached to the products or services of a particular organization, distinguishing them from the goods of its competitors. To customers and patients, a brand conjures up whatever images or associations they have about the organization from reading, talking to their friends, or their own experiences. In that sense, companies are constantly remaking their brands with every customer interaction and every public stance. In healthcare, as elsewhere, the importance of this activity cannot be over emphasized. People recognize their healthcare organizations by their brands.

Building a brand into a strong asset can be truly difficult in this over-crowded and hyper-competitive marketplace. Moreover, its strength can be lost in the blink of an eye — or a single malpractice accusation. A winning brand is a superb, enduring asset and should be protected. Care must be taken, for example, to see that any program intended to make the most of a brand doesn't mar its reputation in the process.

One of the most admired brands in all of healthcare is the Mayo Clinic, in Rochester, Minnesota.

Who: Mayo Clinic.
How: It expanded its brand.

Founded by two physicians, William and Charles Mayo, in the late 1800s, the clinic is one of the largest integrated group practices in the world, with more than 2,000 physicians. Its special strength is its ability to diagnose and treat almost any kind of medical problem. The Mayo Clinic's brand conjures up words and phrases such as "comprehensive," "exhaustive," and "no stone unturned."

Years ago, the organization began creating value with its brand asset by replicating itself in new locations, specifically Jacksonville, Florida and Scottsdale, Arizona. The three sites care for more than 400,000 patients a year.

Beyond that, the Mayo Clinic has extended its brand through a variety of books and newsletters. The *Mayo Clinic Family Health Book*, for example, with 500 illustrations, has sold more than a million copies. There are Mayo Clinic books on chronic pain, high blood pressure, and arthritis, and even a cookbook produced with retailer Williams-Sonoma. The newsletters focus on specific issues, such as women's health, or cover general health topics, such as aging.

In addition to its consumer publishing, the clinic has been working to extend its brand online since 1995. Its most recent Internet offerings have been twofold. Health Oasis offers the public and physicians free access to articles edited by doctors from the Mayo Clinic. HealthQuest provides a wide range of health information to companies that have signed up for the service. Employees of these companies can access the site on a 24-hour-a-day basis and learn the most recent developments on ailments that may be affecting them or their families.

Now the clinic has decided to replace Health Oasis and HealthQuest

With its new Web project, the Mayo Clinic is staking its claim as the premier healthcare information site on the Internet.

with a single new site that will significantly expand Mayo's online services and strengthen its brand assets. The new site is a for-profit venture financed separately from the clinic, which eliminates the financial limitations imposed by Mayo's non-profit status. Revenues Mayo receives will support medical research.

"We will provide the user with one-stop shopping for information, and interactive tools to monitor his or her own health," said Dr. Brooks Edwards, a Mayo Clinic cardiologist and medical editor of MayoClinic.com. The site also features executive and community features, such as chat rooms and message boards for users to discuss health issues.

With this project, Mayo is staking its claim as the premier healthcare information site on the Internet, which seems appropriate for an organization that maintains a reputation as a pioneer in the medical field. Or, as we might express it, the new Web site will help Mayo burnish its brand asset, and, in so doing, create new value. It is another conduit for keeping its brand in the public eye.

Proprietary Knowledge.
We would be remiss if we did not at least touch on proprietary knowledge as an asset of the utmost value today. One Cambridge, Massachusetts-based company, Millennium Pharmaceuticals, Inc., is certain that its proprietary knowledge and intellectual property are valuable assets, and makes sure to convey that commitment to its investors, employees, and customers who reward the organization for its unyielding pursuit of them.

Who: Millennium Pharmaceuticals, Inc.
How: It converts discoveries into intellectual property.

In December 1999, only days away from Y2K, the aptly named Millennium scored a major coup when it acquired U.S. Patent No. 5,972,621 related to its work in understanding obesity and the diseases it causes. Surpassing its rivals in pharmaceutical, biotechnology, and academic organizations, Millennium converted a discovery in the field of obesity research into proprietary knowledge.

Millennium is on the leading edge as a discoverer and developer of drugs. Through acquisitions and a series of strategic alliances, it has achieved a position of influence in the notoriously precarious biopharmaceutical industry in only 7 short years. Starting out with 30 researchers in 1993, Millennium now counts more than 1,200 scientists, managers, and technicians in its ranks.

This elite group works to decipher the roles of genes in certain diseases. Using its own innovative science and technology platforms, Millennium seeks to accelerate the process of sifting through the human genome. The overall project is to identify all the genes that relate to disease so that researchers can discover new ways to treat and cure them.

To date, Millennium's work has focused on three main areas: oncolo-

"Just as the price of a textbook is not determined

by the cost of the paper of its pages,

and the price of a computer program

is not determined by the cost of a disk's material,

the price of a medicine is not based on the cost

of its ingredients. The price of a medicine,

like that of other products that result

from research and creativity, is determined

by the knowledge necessary to discover

and develop the drug — knowledge that prevents

and cures disease and relieves suffering,

knowledge that does not come cheaply."

— Raymond V. Gilmartin,
chairman, president, and chief executive officer, Merck & Company, Inc.

gy, inflammation, and metabolic disease. It is trying to produce diagnostics and therapeutics for a variety of conditions, but its current focus is on obesity.

Toward that end, Millennium's scientists have identified more than a dozen genes related to weight regulation. The latest patent is the first issued by the United States covering methods for using the *leptin* receptor to discover new drugs for weight reduction. This marks Millennium's thirteenth patent in the area of obesity.

It is widely understood that the leptin pathway is a key to controlling body weight. Referring to its latest patent as "a significant impediment to competitors," Millennium hopes to unlock the potential of the pathway by discovering drugs that can regulate body weight. Needless to say, such a discovery would be enormously beneficial to patients and be profitable as well.

Millennium has more than 140 U.S. patents in its portfolio, as well as a number of pending applications. Each represents a potential building block to strengthen its fortress of proprietary knowledge, which, in turn, should translate into increased value for Millennium shareholders.

▶ What's Next?

Having suggested how all five of today's sources of value are used in the business models of some the world's most successful companies, we will now expand our focus. In the next chapter, we discuss how to use all five sources of value to build winning business models.

Questions to ask yourself.

Business Model: Consider your company's organization assets. Is it effectively managing and investing in all or many of these assets to create value? How does your business use these assets to link with all its others to form a coherent whole? Here, we include its financial and brick-and-mortar assets, as well as its employee, supplier, and customer assets.

Risks: Do the case studies in this chapter suggest guidelines for determining the organization assets with which your company feels most comfortable taking risks? Does the chapter show some of the ways in which your business is actually creating undue risk by not actively managing and investing in these assets?

Technology: What are best practices in your industry when it comes to linking your organization assets? How do your competitors use the Internet and e-commerce to derive further benefit from their organization assets?

Measurement: How does your company track and measure the value-creating contribution of its organization assets? Does it have a knowledge-management system? Has it installed a management system for its inventory of intellectual property as it has for its inventory of products and services?

PART **3** HOW CAN YOU MANAGE THE ASSETS AND RELATIONSHIPS THAT MATTER NOW?

In Part 1 of this book, we argued

that regardless of the measurement system, healthcare
businesses often invest their time and money in an
array of assets and relationships, and do so without
a clear plan. By making these investments, an
organization creates value and reduces risk — or the
reverse. Therefore, according to our research, those
decisions determine success or failure.

In Part 2, we used case studies from the healthcare industry

to show how some organizations are managing all
their sources of value: physical, financial, and
organization assets and relationships with customers,
employees, and suppliers.

Now, in Part 3, we explain

in detail the four rules that can help your company

create value now.

1. See and build your business model.

2. Take and manage risk like an astute investor.

3. Connect the sources of value you own with those

you don't.

4. Measure and manage all your sources of value.

Let's take a look at who's managing what matters now.

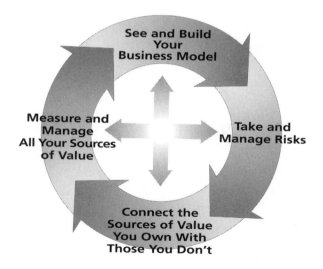

9
SEE AND BUILD YOUR BUSINESS MODEL.

What is the unique combination of assets and relationships that will enable your organization to grow even though it is surrounded by competitors who want to take those sources of value away from you?

> *"Cherish forever what makes you unique,*
> *'cuz you're really a yawn if it goes."*
> — Bette Midler.

In the 1950s, a pair of cardiologists in San Francisco, California, had an annoying problem. The chairs in their waiting room were constantly in need of repair. They finally consulted with an upholsterer

who was amazed at the particular way their patients had misused the chairs. Instead of being worn out evenly, the seats and arms were torn up only along the front few inches. The patients were literally sitting — and fidgeting — on the edge of their seats.

Eventually, the cardiologists, Meyer Friedman and Ray Rosenman, realized that the tendency of their cardiology patients to wear out chairs differently from other kinds of patients was just the beginning. They recognized that their patients had entire patterns of behavior that were idiosyncratic.

There was, the cardiologists hypothesized, a relationship between heart disease and the personality traits of its sufferers.

Friedman and Rosenman fathered the personality classifications, type A and type B, which caught on and spread throughout popular culture in the 1960s. Type As, they said, are "joyless strivers" who tend to be unusually competitive, combative, impatient, hostile, and insecure. On the other hand, type Bs tended to be more patient, calm, noncombative, and emotionally secure. The cardiologists' 1971 study showed that type As were twice as likely to develop coronary-artery disease as type Bs.

Since then, the medical establishment has accepted and extended their work. Type-A behavior — particularly hostility and a quickness to anger — has been shown to be as bad for your heart as cigarette smoking. If, on a regular basis, your blood pressure rises when you are unavoidably annoyed, say, by slow traffic or a rude salesperson, it will, over time, damage your cardiovascular system.

The type A/type B personality distinction has been relevant to thousands of people. And what is true of individuals is, to no small degree, true of organizations — including yours. Like people, companies differ from each other in terms of their business models. And, as we pointed out earlier, how a company invests in its assets and relationships will establish its business model. You express your company's personality through the assets and relationships you choose and how you support and manage their interactions.

Now: Build portfolios of tangible assets.
Next: See and build portfolios of assets and relationships.

The type A/type B descriptions of personalities are not precise. Again, imitative of people, companies are too complex to fit within such neatly drawn categories. In fact, in the case of a company, the personality preference is not limited to type A or type B, rather, it runs the gamut within the five Value Dynamics categories. But a company has a clear behavioral identity, a tendency, just as surely as an investor who is choosing stocks and bonds for an investment portfolio. Organizations are, after all, composed of people who are making decisions according to their organizations' preferences, as well as their own. The assets and relationships an organization values and invests in reflect its collective preferences over time.

Leaders make decisions to acquire and own resources, ranging from physical assets (such as hospitals or new clinics); employee and supplier relationships (with nurses, physician partners, and supply-chain companies); financial assets (equity and debt financing); organization assets (with patents and processes that can be licensed); and customer relationships (new buyers or channels).

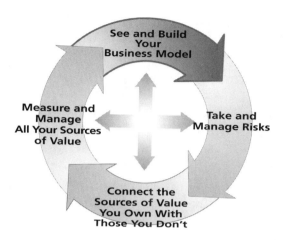

Earnings and profit margins indicate the value realized by these investment choices, as does value creation, all of which are reflected in the marketplaces' evaluations of your organization. If your company is publicly traded, stockholders generate market value. If your company is private or not-for-profit, lenders who provide capital at certain rates, institutional investors, or communities that vote on bond issues assess the value by risk. In these direct and indirect ways, investors rate an organization's investment policies as well as its ability to implement those policies and manage its portfolio. High on their list of desirable assets is the amount of cash a company realizes.

We do not mean to suggest that a company's preference for one or another asset or set of relationships leads to its ignoring all the others. Organizations use all of the sources of value in their companies' business models. They simply tend to put greater weight on some of them.

We are reminded of the question once posed by some wise men: "What's more important to a plant: sun, air, water, or soil?" The right answer is none; they are equally important. If there is too much sun, the plant will burn up; too much water, the plant will drown. What is needed is just the right amount of each. And that goes for sources of value in a business model, as well.

We are not suggesting that a company with a preference for one set of assets or relationships will always and forever maintain that preference.

Conditions change, leadership changes. But, in general and over the long haul, we have found that these preferences do exist. They are what a company and its managers feel most comfortable and natural doing. It's what they have "always done."

Recognizing your company's preferences is not a simple matter. To do so, you need to accept the role that each of your sources of value plays as indicated by the Value Dynamics Framework. Beyond that, though, you may have to detect hidden preferences. Your company may be on auto-pilot and not regularly examining its support of one or another asset or relationship. It may also have preferences that, in the dynamic interactions within an asset-and-relationship portfolio, are destroying rather than creating value.

It is absolutely essential that healthcare leaders see and build their business models — their business genome — and that means understanding their value-creating preferences. In this chapter, we offer our insights and tools to help you see and build a better business model.

See Your Business Model.

To begin with, we should acknowledge that there already exist a variety of methods for measuring an organization and identifying its preferences and corporate personality type. Size, for example, whether it is judged by revenues, sales, earnings, or market capitalization can be measured. In fact, size is important because it is a factor in whether or not you can command a market. On the other hand, it also fosters bureaucracies that make it harder to adapt to market changes. In any event, size, per se, is only one aspect of corporate personality.

> The way your company creates its business model will, more than any other single factor, decide its success or failure, just as it does for individual investors.

Industry designations are another means of categorizing a company. But as companies consolidate and the boundaries around industries are erased, the codes become less and less meaningful.

There are other sources of data about companies that can be used to type them. Trading on the stock markets produces a huge statistical base detailing a company's financial performance. Purchases by customers generate information about the consumer markets. People in the labor mar-

Bricks and clicks or customers and employees can be aligned to create a powerful business model using up-to-date technologies.

ket create information about employment. Government requirements draw forth proxies and other invaluable data. We also have some general perceptions as to preference types. Organizations in the service sector tend to hire more employees, while those on the retail side prefer to build and open more stores. All of these answers address the problem of measurement, but they don't suffice.

When all is said and done, there exists no tool or combination of tools with which managers can envision the identities and interactions of all of their firms' assets and relationships in real time. That is why Andersen has developed its unique approach, which we call Value Imaging.

Discover Your Value Image.

An organization's personality type, its preferences, can change over time, though businesses probably change their personas less easily and less often than people, which is not good. Most healthcare companies must shift their personalities and preferences if they are to achieve success in the changing economic environment.

As you will see in the accompanying graphic, the visualization tool we call Value Imaging starts out as an elaboration on the Value Dynamics Framework, with one or another of the five sources of value receiving more or less investment and support in general. But that is just the beginning of our imaging process. There is a great deal of discipline that accompanies it.

Since there is no agreed upon measurement scheme to weigh many of the sources of value that are most important in the current economy, it is difficult to accurately determine the amount of value that relationships with suppliers or employees contribute to an organization. There are ways to meet that challenge. We look to the information associated with a particular asset or relationship. For customers, it might include retention rates and spending ratios; for employees, turnover rates, and for suppliers, quality ratings and inventory reduction rates.

This data, in conjunction with the Value Dynamics Framework, will reflect the decisions your company has made as to which sources of value it invests in and which it does not. And by keeping that information up to date, you can visualize just how your assets and relationships are interacting, and to what effect.

After all, you cannot change what you cannot see. If you are going to be able to manage your company's sources of value effectively, you need to be able to visualize just how the company is investing in its assets and relationships and how the financial markets are rewarding those investments.

When the time comes to think about changing your business model — a time, we submit, that is inevitable — you can actually use Value Imaging to see how your model would change with different investment decisions. What we offer is not precise. Value Imaging is less like a global positioning system, and more like a compass — it indicates the direction to be taken.

Now, let's take a look at the Value Image of one of the companies we featured earlier: Walgreen Company, based in Deerfield, Illinois

Who: Walgreen Company.
How: It creates value with all its assets and relationships.

Figure 9.1 shows all of Walgreen's sources of value, displayed by our

Fig. 9.1 Walgreen

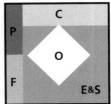

Value Imaging tool. Note that, although we have previously discussed Walgreen primarily in terms of its physical assets, all five sources of value are represented here — in fact, Walgreen's employee and supplier relationships contribute more value than its physical assets.

How so? Value Imaging reflects value creation not solely according to the dollars invested in tangible assets, but in terms of the value derived from the different assets and relationships in a portfolio. In effect, Value Imaging shows Walgreen as investors attempt to see it — that is, with a view toward all of its sources of value. This is the anatomy of the company's market capitalization, not its book value.

Clearly, investors place the highest value on Walgreen's employee and supplier relationships, but each category is important and none can be overlooked. In any company, long-term success depends on how they work together to create value.

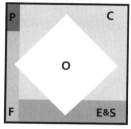

Fig. 9.2 Medtronic

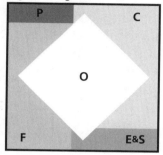

Fig. 9.3 Amgen

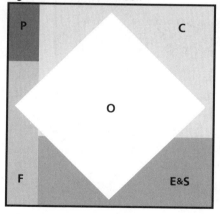

Fig. 9.4 Johnson & Johnson

Value Imaging can help you answer three key questions: What individual assets and relationships are you investing in? What assets and relationships are the markets rewarding? What combinations of assets and relationships are the markets rewarding?

As we did for Walgreen, we applied Value Imaging to all companies discussed earlier in the book (see Figures 9.2, 9.3, and 9.4). You will see that they are creating value not just from the sources of value we focused on, but from their other assets and relationships as well. That only makes sense, of course, since a company is a portfolio of assets and relationships and you need to see them all, individually and as an interacting entity.

In addition to suggesting where the value lies among your sources of value, Value Imaging also provides an ongoing guide to changes in the market's attitude toward your assets and relationships. When the Value Image indicates that the market is rewarding some asset and relationship combinations more than others, you can adjust your portfolio to create greater value, which is, after all, the name of the game. We have found that, in terms of value creation, industry designation matters less than asset combinations.

Build Your Business Model

Harry Markowitz was a 25-year-old graduate student at the University of Chicago when he wrote a seminal paper about securities investment for the *Journal of Finance*. In that paper, "Portfolio Selection," Markowitz confirmed the wisdom of investors who avoid putting all their eggs in one basket. He proved that investing in a variety of companies reduces volatility and increases returns.

With scholarly rigor, Markowitz examined a portfolio of securities in its entirety, applying statistics to understand how the portfolio's inherent risks and returns related to the risks and returns of each individual security. In effect, he asked: How can an investor construct a portfolio of assets that will enhance its overall return and, at the same time, reduce risk?

Markowitz argued that there was an infinite number of risk-and-return combinations, and that some were preferable to others. Thus, the challenge for any investor is to select assets that will strengthen, while simultaneously offsetting, the risks posed by others. When he was awarded the Nobel Prize, *The New York Times* wrote, "It was Dr. Markowitz who refined the economic logic of diversification and offered a practical way to choose an 'optimal portfolio' of assets."

Markowitz explained that an investor's success in maximizing return and minimizing risk, depend on the person's ability to combine assets — that is, the securities of different companies. Though Markowitz focused on portfolios held by individual investors, much of his theory of diversification is relevant to the way companies manage their own assets and relationships.

The decisions and choices you make as you construct your company's business model, some of which may be intentional, others unwitting, comprise your healthcare business's investment policy. The key to success, whether you are a solo practitioner, or a giant pharmaceutical company, is the capacity to change that policy by investing in new combinations of assets and relationships.

Remember, when it comes to sources of value, a portfolio of assets and relationships is potentially greater than the sum of its parts: One plus one can equal much more than two if sources of value are in sync — and much less than two if they are not.

Put another way, your company's investment policy reflects the time and money that the organization spends on the assets and relationships it believes create value and reduce risk. How the company implements those decisions is the next step. Indeed, when you look at your company's portfolio, note that all operating decisions — hiring or firing employees, securing tax exempt financing or selling stock, adding to or diminishing its holdings of property and equipment, resolving whether or not to advertise — are all investment decisions, whether or not they are called that. In other words, in this context, there is no difference between the operating decisions that are enacted and the annual capital planning expenditures.

How does all this affect the redesign of your business model? Or, if your company is a start-up, how does this influence its initial design? No doubt your organization spends (or will spend) large amounts of time and energy defining its strategy, then deciding how to implement it using a host of technologies and performance measurement tools. We urge that your investment policies and risk strategies come first.

We aren't suggesting that you stop what you are doing now. *Product and market strategies still count. But, according to our research, investment and risk strategies count more.* From our experiences with thousands of clients worldwide, both inside and outside the healthcare industry, we are convinced that businesses have focused on the how to the detriment of the what. This is apparent when we ask leaders what kind of activities consume their time. Most of them list the following:

- Delivering products and services to our customers to meet their wants and needs.
- Deciding which systems, technologies, and processes will best insure the on-time delivery of our products and services.
- Choosing which performance measures will most efficiently insure that our workers are doing what we expect of them.

By concentrating on these concerns, some healthcare leaders are actually undermining their businesses and the performance of their investments. Without realizing it, they are becoming more efficient at activities that have less value and relevance. In so doing, they may achieve some short-term growth in current revenues, earnings, and assets, but that road can lead to failure in the long term. Why? Because they may be overlooking the importance of investing in the assets and relationships of tomorrow.

So, when you think about building your business model, keep these three facts in mind:

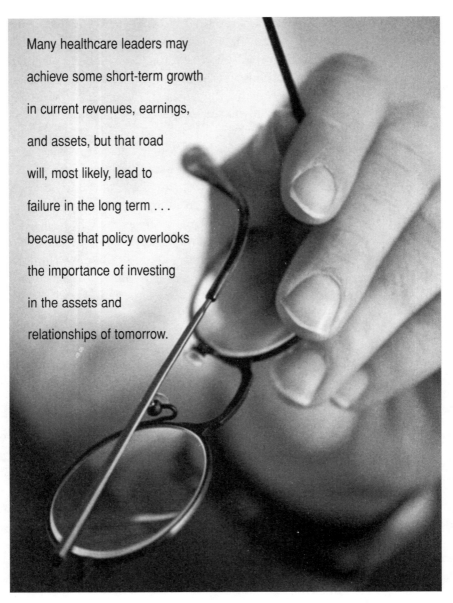

Many healthcare leaders may achieve some short-term growth in current revenues, earnings, and assets, but that road will, most likely, lead to failure in the long term . . . because that policy overlooks the importance of investing in the assets and relationships of tomorrow.

❶ The risk-and-reward ratio of different sources of value is changing. Our research shows that tangible and intangible sources of value are converging in terms of their inherent risks and rewards. And this is a new phenomenon because tangible sources of value have been considered less risky until very recently.

2 Though relationships can begin and end quickly today, they are the key to value creation. Physical assets or "fixed" investments have always been regarded as less risky than intangibles, such as relationships with employees or customers. Tangible assets, increasingly commoditized, are not as important for creating competitive advantage.

3 In today's world, technology is about more than speed and efficiency. It enables new and valuable connections and relationships.

To insure that your business model possesses the right combination and proportion of assets and relationships, follow this approach to ignite a value revolution in your organization:

1. Identify all your sources of value.

Identify all of your sources of value by organizing them into five categories. Then, subdivide your assets and relationships along two dimensions: tangible versus intangible, and owned versus unowned. For example, some buildings are tangible and owned; intellectual capital is intangible and owned; relationships with customers are intangible and unowned. The resulting matrix helps you to plot all of your assets.

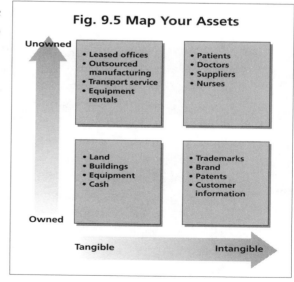

Fig. 9.5 Map Your Assets

Unowned
- Leased offices
- Outsourced manufacturing
- Transport service
- Equipment rentals

- Patients
- Doctors
- Suppliers
- Nurses

- Land
- Buildings
- Equipment
- Cash

- Trademarks
- Brand
- Patents
- Customer information

Owned

Tangible   *Intangible*

2. Estimate the value of your assets and relationships.

First, examine how your organization distributes its time and spends its money among its assets and relationships. Next, estimate the value extracted from those investments — that is, the return on investment. Eventually, more sophisticated tools and systems will allow you to measure your organization's sources of value with advanced precision, enabling you to improve the value of your asset mix even further.

3. Identify what combination of assets and relationships will produce the most value.

Business is all about producing profits and value. Your organization's mission and goals need to be coordinated with the sources of value that will achieve objectives most effectively. Ideally, you can identify what assets and relationships you require and how, specifically, to make the most of them.

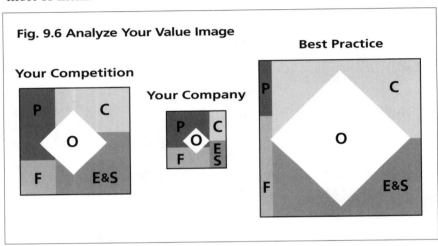

Fig. 9.6 Analyze Your Value Image

Your Competition

Your Company

Best Practice

▶ **Remember:** Not all business models are created equal. Sources of value and the technologies, systems, and processes that connect them are changing. If your organization's history includes owning most of its sources of value, keep in mind the increasingly popular option of acquiring an asset without actually buying and owning it. Partners can provide and continue to manage particular assets that you can offer to your customers. Indeed, many investors today prefer companies that are involved in innovative alliances that allow those organizations to create added value through flexible asset management arrangements without deploying more capital. Innovative alliances have the potential to generate heretofore untapped, valuable opportunities for healthcare organizations.

4. Rebalance your asset and relationship portfolio.

Companies of all types create their business models by acquiring, renewing, and disposing of assets and relationships, though the process may not be formally structured to encompass certain intangible assets. To scale the heights of success, though, an action plan should include a diversified portfolio of assets and relationships. This portfolio must be constantly realigned with the marketplace so that your company is constantly fine-tuning its investment policy and the assets and relationships in which it invests.

Every source of value has unique financing and management requirements. This is quite clear with tangible assets: A building, for example, can be financed and disposed of through a variety of transactions singular to that building. Significantly, the same rule applies to intangible assets, such as intellectual property. Those assets also have unique financing and management requirements.

To rebalance your business model intelligently, you must determine the fair value of all your assets and relationships, and how those values are changing. To do this, you need access to financial, operating (including intellectual capital), and budgeting skills to ensure that all sources of value are priced accurately and managed cost-effectively.

► **Remember:** Building your company's business model is a dynamic and perpetually changing process. There is no source of value available to any organization in any industry that is not also available to your healthcare enterprise. To compete today, every company must tap the same sources of value, including relationships with customers, employees, and suppliers. The question for your company is this: How are you going to form the most valuable alliances when the competition for them is intense from both visible and invisible competitors?

▶ What's Next?

Risk is a fact of life, especially when you vie for sources of value, such as relationships with customers, employees, and investors. If technology has not altered our vulnerabilities to risk, it has surely changed our abilities to manage it. As the next chapter makes clear, controlling risk is as germane to your company's success as any facet of the business model.

Questions to ask yourself:

Business Model: Does your company carefully and frequently monitor the logic behind its investment decisions, or does it simply rely on past practices?

Risk: The challenge for all investors, businesses included, is to determine their risk tolerance. Does your company have an explicit policy to accomplish that or is risk management buried deep in the finance department, where there may be little recognition that intangible assets and relationships create risk and balance return?

Technology: New technologies that enable and enhance specific types of assets and relationships are being developed. Customer relationship management software and intellectual capital management software are examples. Is your company using the technologies that are necessary for success?

Measurement: Do you have measurement systems that allow you to track the contributions that all your assets and relationships make to your company's performance? If not, can you account for the time and capital you spend on each?

10 TAKE AND MANAGE RISK LIKE AN ASTUTE INVESTOR.

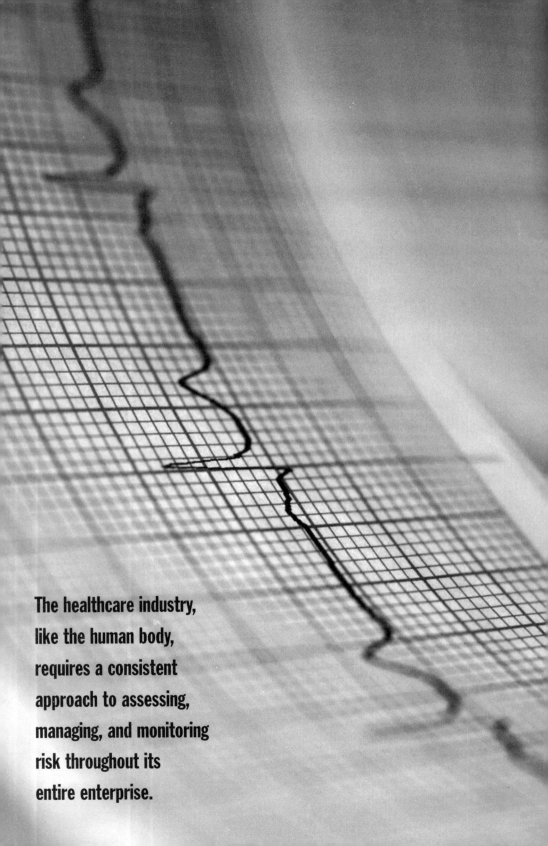

The healthcare industry, like the human body, requires a consistent approach to assessing, managing, and monitoring risk throughout its entire enterprise.

For six centuries, the Roman army marched across the Western world, creating an empire that would eventually encompass most of Europe, the Middle East, and North Africa.

Warfare at the time consisted of the face-to-face clash of opposing armies until one side backed down and fled. What made the Roman army so formidable was its capacity to engage its enemies without flinching — and without yielding an inch.

In that era, Roman generals' greatest risk was their soldiers' instinct to run from danger and the threat of death. The generals' ability to manage that risk, to find ways to keep their troops engaged in battle, to a large part, determined the extent and longevity of the Roman Empire.

In part, the Roman soldiers' steadfastness can be attributed to the armies' high level of organization. Each soldier belonged to a unit of

10 men, which, in turn, belonged to a group of 100 units, which then became part of a legion made up of 6,000 infantrymen and 200 cavalrymen. The loyalties within the smaller units produced a cohesion that helped ensure discipline in combat.

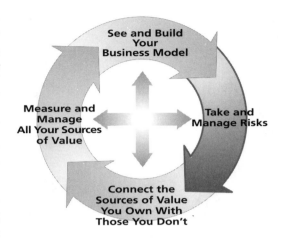

Roman generals had other ways of managing their chief risk. Any unit of soldiers that retreated prematurely was "decimated" — 1 out of every 10 of its members, chosen by drawing lots, was beaten to death by the other soldiers. On the other hand, bravery was rewarded. A legionary who killed an enemy soldier might be given a drinking bowl.

Like all effective leaders in the boardroom and on the battlefield, the generals recognized the need to revise their risk-management strategies according to changing circumstances.

In the early years, the armies of Rome were made up of citizen voters who served for a limited time, then returned to their farms and families. When the Romans invaded Spain in the third century B.C., however, the legions were too far from home to be regularly relieved. To recruit soldiers willing to fight indefinitely, the generals had to pay them — not just with salaries, but with a share of the spoils of war.

Leaders who can accurately calculate and manage the risks involved in a course of action usually carry the day.

Isolated from their homes, the mercenaries developed a powerful *esprit de corps*. They fought magnificently, but their loyalties were less to the Roman community as a whole than to themselves and the leaders who rewarded them, and that created a risk that Roman leaders had not anticipated.

As H.G. Wells described in *The Outline of History*, before the Punic Wars, ambitious politicians courted the voters; after the wars, they courted the legions. It was the beginning of the end of the Roman Republic.

Leaders who can accurately calculate and manage the risks involved in a course of action usually carry the day. And that is as relevant today as it was in ancient Rome. The development of civilization, including commerce, can be traced to our evolving skill at doing just that.

Centuries ago, traders and merchants found ways to minimize the danger to their physical and financial assets. For instance, when gold bullion and other precious goods had to be transported across oceans, they divided them among several ships to reduce potential loss if one or more ships failed to complete the voyage.

They also created insurance markets to guard physical and financial assets against risk. Lloyds of London, for example, originated in Edward Lloyd's coffee house beside the Thames River when seventeenth-century merchants and captains gathered to insure ships and their cargoes. Each man who took a share of a risk put his name on the insurance policy, one under the other, along with the amount he agreed to cover. They were known as "underwriters."

Now: Manage the risks that are associated with tangible assets.
Next: Manage the risks that are associated with assets and relationships.

Insurers are still called underwriters, but the sources of value in today's world have expanded to include assets and relationships that extend beyond an organization's financial and physical holdings. The problem is that risk management has failed to keep pace. By and large, it still focuses on tangible assets.

In this chapter, we offer a solution. We show you how to redesign your company's approach to managing risk so that you will make the most of the sources of value that matter in today's economy.

As we pointed out in the previous chapter, effective enterprise-wide risk management is essential to realizing your business' goals. In the pages ahead, we present a three-part framework that can help you organize your thoughts about risk, along with an analysis of two companies using that framework. We also present a seven-step program for examining and improving your company's method of risk management. First, let's take a fresh look at business risk along three dimensions (see Figure 10.1).

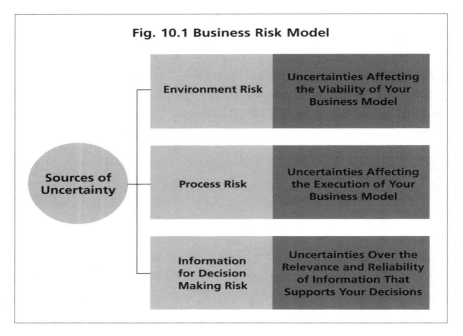

Fig. 10.1 Business Risk Model

Sources of Uncertainty

Environment Risk — Uncertainties Affecting the Viability of Your Business Model

Process Risk — Uncertainties Affecting the Execution of Your Business Model

Information for Decision Making Risk — Uncertainties Over the Relevance and Reliability of Information That Supports Your Decisions

❶ Environment risk.

These risks are caused by external forces that affect an organization's performance. Examples are new technologies, new competitors, and new regulations. Environment risks can cause elements of your business model to become obsolete or ineffective.

❷ Process risk.

These risks arise when business processes and technologies fail to achieve their objectives or are overlooked. Examples range from a shortage of raw materials and skilled workers to equipment breakdowns and loss of key suppliers.

❸ Information for decision-making risk.

These risks surface when the information upon which business decisions are made is incomplete, out of date, inaccurate, or irrelevant. Examples include a company's inability to monitor and measure its processes; its leaders' inability to stay informed about prospective regulatory changes; or managers' failure to spot a competitor's initiative before it is too late.

How should healthcare companies make sure they consider all three risk factors when they design their business models? Our answer is in the form of detailed risk-reward analyses of two organizations, one in financial services, the other in healthcare.

The first company is the credit-card giant Capital One Financial Corporation of Falls Church, Virginia. The other is Harvard Pilgrim Health Care, Inc., the largest HMO in Massachusetts. Though worlds apart in their lines of business, locations, and cultures, these two companies share similar asset and relationship configurations from which opportunities and risks arise.

Our focus is on the risks attending organization assets and relationships with customers, employees, and suppliers. Since the risks connected with maximizing physical and financial assets are well-known and documented, we do not emphasize them here — with the understanding that they must not be neglected when you think about your company's business model.

▶ **One further thought:** The task of managing the risks attached to your business model and its component assets and relationships will be incomplete if you fail to include those assets and relationships that are not part of your company. The sources of value you own engender internal, controlled risks; those you do not own engender external, uncontrolled risks.

With those caveats, let's proceed to our two examples of risk management.

Who: Capital One Financial Corporation.
How: It manages the risks associated with its sources of value.

"I put heavy weight on certainty," Warren E. Buffett, chairman and chief executive officer of Berkshire Hathaway, Inc., famously observed. "If you do that, the whole idea of a risk factor doesn't make any sense to me. . . . Risk comes from not knowing what you are doing."

Certainty has never accompanied the bold innovations of Capital One's Richard D. Fairbank, chairman and chief executive officer, and Nigel W. Morris, cofounder and president. But they do have a weapon that comes close: They test everything — not only their products, processes, and job applicants, but also their customers and longtime employees.

When Capital One plans an action, it assesses the risks carefully and on occasion, shies away from bad ideas. More often, the company refuses to allow risk to blind it to great opportunity. Whatever its final decision, the company regards the very process of evaluating risk as a boost to its knowledge. "Very few companies have the ability to test and learn," Morris has noted. Capital One is among those that do.

When Fairbank and Morris surprised the industry by introducing two blockbuster ideas, Capital One was still part of Signet Banking Corporation. (It went public in 1994.) Both ideas were intended to increase the value of the company's customer asset.

One innovation was the teaser-rate card, which sought to lure consumers away from more established cards by offering temporarily, lowered interest rates. The second was the balance-transfer option, which gave new customers a chance to transfer balances they had with other cards to a single Capital One account. The balance transfer was intended to attract new customers and, simultaneously, to increase the size of the average customer's monthly interest payment.

From the perspective of enterprise-wide risk management, these efforts were subject to all three types of risk — environment, process, and information for decision-making.

Capital One was concerned that competitors would copy either or both the teaser rate and the balance transfer programs. That environment risk was particularly high for the teaser rate, which had the potential to ignite a rate war that could wipe out earnings across the industry.

Because the teaser rate offered such thin margins, the pressure on the company's processes to perform at peak efficiency was far greater than usual, with little, if any, room for error. A breakdown in the underwriting or delivery processes had to be avoided before the margins turned negative. The enormous number of new customers attracted by the low rate represented yet another kind of process risk — the company's capacity to serve and retain the massive influx.

Another risk inherent in both the teaser-rate and the balance-transfer initiatives was that information for decision-making would not be developed and disseminated quickly enough. Failure was likely if, for example, the financial data underlying the strategies changed, or the methods for measuring new customers' credit worthiness were faulty. Another risk was that competitors might swiftly undercut Capital One's rates without decision-makers hearing about it in sufficient time to design a counter-strategy.

Though aware of these three dangers, Fairbank and Morris concluded that the opportunities far outweighed the risks. They were convinced that the two programs could lure millions of consumers away from the leading credit-card companies, and they were right.

Eventually, however, the environment risks we discussed became realities, and Capital One began to lose customers. Rivals not only copied Capital's innovations; they also inadvertently created a new breed of cardholder — the "teaser-hopper," who stayed with a card only as long as the low rate was effective, then signed up for another company's teaser rate.

Confident that most consumers did not enjoy teaser-hopping, Capital One devoted two years to testing various fixed-rate, no-annual-fee cards. The organization actually discovered a rate that pleased just about every consumer, though it had one fatal weakness: It failed to yield a profit.

The company solved that problem by narrowing its target. It began by offering a version of its "perfect" card (with a 9.9 percent annual interest rate) to just one segment of the market: those consumers least likely to default. The results were so favorable that the company dispensed with teaser-rate cards altogether and learned a valuable lesson: Environment risks can overtake even the most careful and ingenious innovators.

Today, Capital One has approximately 30 million customers and ranks among the top 10 credit-card issuers in the United States. Still, the organization never rests. It is constantly inventing new products, currently offering more than 6,000 different kinds of credit cards, and continuing to conduct its business in innovative ways.

Some of the company's most impressive breakthroughs have been aimed at creating the most value with its employees. In the view of chairman Fairbank, "Credit cards aren't banking — they're information." Under his leadership, the company gathered vast quantities of information about its customers and combined it with state-of-the-art technology. As a result, telephone agents are provided appropriate information that prepares them for a specific customer's questions before they even hear his or her voice on the line.

As soon as the customer finishes dialing, Capital One's computers determine the caller's identity, the likely reason for the call, and the agent who can best respond. That agent receives a computer screen full of data on the customer along with suggestions on how to deal with the probable purpose of the call. In addition, the data includes a prediction of what products the customer may be interested in buying.

Telephone agents are provided appropriate information that prepares them for a specific customer's questions before they even hear his or her voice on the line.

That kind of cross-selling was a revolutionary development in the industry, and one that the healthcare industry would do well to consider. Just five years ago, Capital One was trying to sell non-credit-card items by phoning its customers or sending them inserts with their bills. When the company examined the results of this method, it found, unsurprisingly, that it was only marginally successful. Someone suggested that the company see how customers reacted to cross-selling when they called on other matters.

Understandably, the internal objections were instant, because the process risks were substantial. Employees who answered the phones considered themselves service specialists, and protested that they would not be good at sales. Many managers agreed that it was impossible to combine the two functions in a single person efficiently while also keeping the calls short enough to be profitable.

The idea also presented environment risks, not the least of which was that competitors could easily hire away the best phone associates (as they are called at Capital One). Yet the potential gains were too high to ignore.

Initially, phone associates tried in-bound cross-selling with customers calling to activate a new card. While they waited for the computer to complete that process, customers were told about the opportunity to consolidate their credit-card debt with Capital One. The technique attracted immediate customer interest.

The company quickly moved to help its phone associates feel more comfortable in their new role as salespeople. The associates felt that if they were expected to discuss products with the customer, they should also have the authority to complete the sale, and the company agreed.

Choosing the right products for cross-selling was itself loaded with risks: The wrong approach could easily alienate new customers. The company settled on relatively safe products, including auto insurance from The Hartford Company, catalog clubs from Damark International, Inc., and long-distance telephone service from MCI.

The cross-selling process was simplified by a sophisticated information-technology system, in which calls from customers considered most likely to buy were routed to associates whose specialty was telephone sales.

Like every organization, Capital One sought to increase the value of its employee assets by hiring the right people. Again, like most other organizations, the company selected applicants largely on the recommendation of the supervisors to whom they would directly report. At Capital One, though, it turned out that the supervisors' ratings failed to correlate with the employees' performance.

It was difficult to know what to do. Excluding supervisors from the hiring process would undoubtedly anger them and might even impair their performances. In Value Dynamics terms, such a decision posed a major process risk, which may have led to an information for decision-making risk if the supervisors were to isolate themselves within the organization. It could also have led to an environment risk if they joined a rival company.

In this case, the company's leaders felt the risk was worth taking and the results proved them right. Capital One has improved its ability to predict the success of new hires, and supervisors have become accustomed to meeting successful job applicants only after they have been hired. In an effort to hone its candidate-selection process even more, Capital One asked hundreds of veteran employees to participate in various pre-employment tests. The company compares these results with its own individual employees' work records to improve the design of the test — that is, to select questions that correlate with high job performance. To be sure, some workers are uncomfortable with these tests, a risk similar to those posed when supervisors were excluded from the hiring process. Process risk is the primary concern here, but discomfort goes with the territory at Capital One. Constantly rejecting convention in favor of innovation, Capital One, though comfortable taking risks, is, at the same time, dedicated to conducting painstaking research and thorough-

Constantly rejecting convention in favor of innovation, Capital One, though **comfortable taking risks,** is, at the same time, dedicated to conducting **painstaking research** and thoroughly examining ideas and concepts in order to reduce risk.

ly examining ideas and concepts to reduce risk. That combination has enabled the company to manage its risks, internal and external, managed and unmanaged, and to prosper in a most competitive industry.

Who: Harvard Pilgrim Health Care, Inc.
How: It underestimated the risks, internal and external, related to its sources of value.

For the first 6 months of 2000, Harvard Pilgrim Health Care — a not-for-profit HMO operating throughout New England — was placed in receivership because unrecorded medical costs and contingent liabilities had exhausted its statutory net worth. The temporary receivership sent shock waves far beyond the HMO's headquarters. As a multi-state HMO, Harvard Pilgrim held 40 percent of the healthcare market in Massachusetts alone.

Size was not the health plan's only advantage. Even more important were its historic associations with Harvard Medical School's teaching hospitals and its consistently high ratings for clinical quality and member satisfaction. Respected throughout New England, Harvard Pilgrim was one of the strongest healthcare brands in the United States.

Harvard Pilgrim's difficulties were not sudden — the company had been losing money for several years. The business was being eaten away by the expense of new medical technologies, escalating prescription-drug costs, pressure from hospitals and physicians, and a competitive environment in which premium increases had to be held to an absolute minimum. The health plan filed formal statements of operating losses of $94 million in 1998 and $96 million for the first three quarters of 1999.

In the spring of 1999, the Harvard Pilgrim board hired a new chief executive officer, Charles D. Baker, who tried to boost statutory net worth by arranging a sale and leaseback of eight affiliated health-center sites. Due diligence surrounding the transaction turned up an unexpected problem: additional unrecorded losses of more than $75 million.

That revelation was disastrous for the new management team and the providers serving Harvard Pilgrim. The Commonwealth of Massachusetts immediately placed the organization in temporary receivership, which, according to many who reported and analyzed the event, left Massachusetts' providers holding hundreds of millions of dollars in stranded assets in accounts receivable "with questionable value from Harvard Pilgrim Health Care."

How could losses of such magnitude remain undiscovered? The answer lies in poor management of our third risk category, information for decision-making risk. That management failure affected not just balance-sheet assets like financial capital and physical properties, but intangible assets as well.

Formed in 1969 as Harvard Community Health Plan, the organization grew rapidly through a series of mergers to become a large and complex enterprise. The mergers, which combined different cultures, also brought together organizations with disparate systems for accounting, contracting, paying claims, and providing membership services. These inconsistencies represented a constant and growing process risk.

The integration problems were compounded in 1995 when Harvard Community Health Plan merged with Pilgrim Health Care, an HMO with dramatically different values, systems, and cultures. Systems and processes failed to mesh, cultures were discordant, and most information for decision-making, when it existed at all, was incomplete. Though Harvard Pilgrim's failure had many fathers, one well-known analyst focused on the financial-information problem, suggesting that the company "seems to have been flying blind."

How is this related to a new view of risk management? We maintain

If Harvard Pilgrim had designed and implemented an enterprise-wide risk-management program, it surely would have **noticed signs of trouble earlier.**

that risk must be managed across all sources of value. If Harvard Pilgrim had designed and implemented an enterprise-wide risk-management program, it surely would have noticed signs of trouble earlier. Identifying and analyzing its environment, process, and information for decision-making risks would have uncovered the particular areas of risk, which, in this case, were related to Harvard Pilgrim's organization assets.

Our message is straightforward: The prognosis for your healthcare

Fig. 10.2 Seven-Step Business-Risk-Management Process

Establish Business Risk Management Process
•Goals and objectives
•Common language
•Oversight structure

Assess Business Risks
•Identify
•Source •Measure

Information for Decision Making

Continuously Improve Risk Management Capabilities

Develop Business Risk Management Strategies
•Avoid •Reduce •Retain
•Exploit •Transfer

Monitor Risk Management Performance

Design/Implement Risk Management Capabilites

company's business model — which is to say, the particular assets and relationships in which it invests — is intimately connected to the risks associated with each of those assets and relationships. Therefore, it is essential that the connections between your company's investment policy and its enterprise-wide risk-management policies be made apparent. We suggest that you consider risk and reward as inextricably entwined, two sides of the same coin. Ultimately, understanding and managing your sources of value from this perspective will be at the core of your success.

In the course of working with dozens of companies, within and beyond the healthcare industry, we have developed a seven-step approach that makes the links between business model and risk explicit (see Figure 10.2).

Let's take each step in turn.

Step 1: Establish a process of managing business risk.

Start by defining the parameters of risk to your enterprise, drawing a bright line between the limits of your goals and the limits of your ability to absorb risk. You will need a management structure, including appropriate roles, systems, and tools.

Step 2: Assess risks.

It is important to identify and prioritize the sources of risk — internal and external, managed and unmanaged — that may accompany your business model. Using Figure 10.3, you can begin to plot your own risks according to these variables.

Remember that various asset and relationship combinations create unique risks, which may exacerbate those precipitated by new, disruptive technologies, bold competitors, complex transactions, converging industries, and emerging markets.

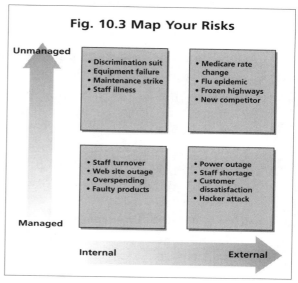

Fig. 10.3 Map Your Risks

Unmanaged

- Discrimination suit
- Equipment failure
- Maintenance strike
- Staff illness

- Medicare rate change
- Flu epidemic
- Frozen highways
- New competitor

- Staff turnover
- Web site outage
- Overspending
- Faulty products

- Power outage
- Staff shortage
- Customer dissatisfaction
- Hacker attack

Managed

Internal   External

Step 3: Set strategy.

To master risk, whether internal or external, managed or unmanaged, clarify your appetite for it. Identify the business model you want to build and the assets and relationships you need to build it.

Step 4: Manage risks.

How will your organization adjust its business model to deal with the risks you identify? It depends on how central the asset or relationship is to your business and how serious the risk is to your success. If an internal risk is not central to the business model, you can transfer it elsewhere (make it external) by outsourcing or partnering, or you can hedge the risk with insurance or derivatives. Remember, certain risks that bother one organization may please another, in which case transferring them creates value for both parties. In other words, risk can be converted into opportunity.

The only certainty is that ignoring risk is guaranteed to create it.

Managing risk is relatively simple. No massive bureaucracy is required. The priority is a steady flow of accurate information that keeps organizations up to date on the status of their plans. Information and Internet technology can connect all your assets and relationships, enabling you to keep track of the three major risks attendant on any business model — environment, process, and information for decision-making.

Step 5: Monitor risk-management activities.

It is important to monitor the effectiveness of your organization's risk-management activities. Do you have a process in place for identifying your enterprise's risks accurately? If not, why not? Have your risk solutions and controls been working? Benchmarking your company against others is a good idea. So, too, is learning from the outcomes (both good and bad) of individual strategic decisions, then eliminating the ones that aren't working.

Step 6: Improve risk-management activities.

Apply what you learn from monitoring to continuously improving how you manage risk.

Step 7: Continuously obtain information.

Finally, remember that the alternative to managing without continuous, complete, and appropriate information is doing so by guesswork, which is tantamount to not managing at all. Information is at the heart of the risk-management.

How can your organization develop a better understanding of its enterprise-wide risk-management skills and requirements? Start by examining how you have invested in your portfolio of assets and relationships. Determine whether your choices are creating the synergy that produces value, or if your company has put too many eggs in one basket — buying and financing more physical assets, for example, or adding to the number of nursing homes in your chain. Such moves may drastically reduce your company's flexibility, and thus its ability to seize opportunities when they appear. Examining your portfolio is crucial, because that is where you will find the roots of opportunities as well as risks.

Risk is a reality of life, and business is constantly changing in today's tumultuous economy. Within that dynamic environment, your strategies for risk management must evolve at the same pace. The healthcare industry must pay more attention to risks. Only then can it protect itself from them. Our proposal is that enterprise-wide risk management becomes an essential part of your company's operations.

Elevating the importance of risk as part and parcel of your company's business model will allow you to create goals that can be shared throughout the organization, and you will maximize the value of all assets and relationships. You can neither manage risk nor use it to your advantage until you recognize it. In an economy characterized by uncertainty and the rising value of intangible assets and relationships, managing risk makes enormous business sense. It can help you harness cutting-edge advances in technology and knowledge.

What is required is a consistent approach to assessing, managing, and monitoring risk throughout and beyond an entire enterprise. Following these recommendations will foster open communication about what matters and what does not — including the issue of taking more risks and reaping more rewards.

Put another way, if enterprise-wide risk management becomes routine, you will see your business model in a new way, with all the successes and flaws that arise from its assets and relationships.

 What's Next?

How can healthcare organizations use state-of-the-art technologies, systems, and processes to deliver unprecedented value to their customers, investors, bondholders, partners, and employees? How can healthcare companies connect the assets they own with those they don't? Those connections are key. In the next chapter, we show how healthcare organizations can create value and achieve competitive advantage by connecting all their assets, external as well as internal, owned as well as unowned. By connecting their assets and relationships, these companies can avoid many of the errors that bedevil the healthcare industry today, and, in this industry, that means saving lives.

Questions to ask yourself.

Business Model: For businesses, as for investors, risk and reward are inseparable. Does your healthcare company understand risk as an integral part of its business model? If you have not already adopted that approach, consider mapping all of the internal and external, managed and unmanaged risks related to all your organizations. That map will tell you where you are and where you need to go.

Risk: Does your company have explicit risk-management techniques for all of your sources of value, and for the three dimensions of risk discussed earlier in the chapter?

Technology: Technology plays a vital role in managing risk, but technologies can themselves destroy or enhance your sources of value. Is your company aware of which internal technologies will strengthen its enterprise-wide risk-management capabilities and which external technologies will alter what you do and how you do it?

Measurement: Measurement is clearly essential for understanding your company's performance and how you are progressing toward achieving your goals — both financial and nonfinancial. Does your company have a measurement and reporting system that keeps score of how well you are doing with risk?

11 CONNECT THE SOURCES OF VALUE YOU OWN WITH THOSE YOU DON'T.

"The Web will be the foundation for a new healthcare industry infrastructure that can support complex, multi-party transactions among empowered consumers, wired practitioners, real-time supply chains, and service-conscious payers."

—*Forrester Research.*

As one of the nation's outstanding healthcare institutions, Massachusetts General Hospital (MGH) has used its prodigious medical expertise to benefit

thousands of patients who travel to its 900-bed Boston facility from around the state and the world. That has been, and remains, the business model of most U.S. hospitals today — a model that tells patients (customers), "This is where we are located. Come by when you're in need."

Today, MGH is beginning to reinvent its business model. More frequently, its message is, "We are wherever you are, and our expertise is available whenever you need it." A company substantially responsible for translating that message into a commercially affordable service is WorldCare, Inc., a Cambridge, Massachusetts-based, pioneer and leader

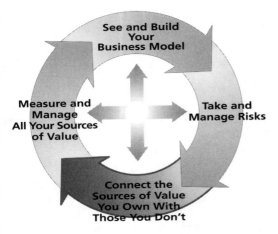

See and Build Your Business Model

Measure and Manage All Your Sources of Value

Take and Manage Risks

Connect the Sources of Value You Own With Those You Don't

in global "e-health" services. Founded in 1994 through a joint venture with MGH, but now privately owned, WorldCare facilitates international access to high-quality U.S. healthcare. It can deliver second medical opinions electronically and provide insurance plans for U.S.-based treatments for serious illnesses. Today, with 17 offices worldwide, WorldCare is assisting The WorldCare Consortium, comprised of The Cleveland Clinic Foundation, Duke University Health System, Johns Hopkins Medicine, and Partners HealthCare System, Inc., which includes MGH and Brigham and Women's Hospital. Its goal is to reach out to patients and providers in every corner of the globe.

WorldCare utilizes a "store and forward" model for the encrypted transmission of medical records, including text and image-based studies such as computed axial tomography (CT), magnetic resonance imaging (MRI), X-ray, and ultrasounds from remote parts of the world to specialists and subspecialists for consultation.

What makes WorldCare's approach even more remarkable is the fact that the consortium is made up of hospitals that have historically been fiercely competitive.

What makes WorldCare's approach even more remarkable is the fact that the consortium is made up of hospitals that have historically been fiercely competitive. Hence, MGH and the other consortium institutions have, in effect, recognized and met our first three challenges: One, they are redesigning their business models to leverage all their assets and relationships. Two, they have calculated the business risks of using — and not using — new technologies. And, three, they have integrated their internal and external sources of value by using whatever systems, processes, and technologies that can help to connect them. The operative word is "connect" — the password to true competitive advantage and value now.

Connectivity is at the heart of this chapter.

Now: Businesses use technology to connect their systems and processes.
Next: Businesses use technology to connect their assets and relationships.

Market imperatives today require companies to redefine value in the most inclusive terms, as opposed to the more exclusive ownership formats of the past. Value is the sum total of the assets and relationships within and outside of a company's walls, and includes relationships and proprietary knowledge, as well as customers and suppliers, which, though perceived as unowned, are crucial nonetheless. What now drives business success is a company's ability to identify and connect all its sources of value. The goal is, of course, to strengthen a company's resources, so that it can apply the resultant power to new opportunities.

In the pages ahead, we discuss how to connect assets and relationships, citing many examples that will be useful to your company. In addition, we examine the healthcare industry's current performance connecting assets and relationships. Sadly, our example of MGH represents only a minority of healthcare facilities. Most trail far behind their counterparts in other industries.

A recent article in the *Harvard Business Review* expressed this point: "The healthcare industry desperately needs to open its doors to market forces . . . to disruptive technologies and business models that may threaten the status quo, but will ultimately raise the quality of healthcare for everyone."

Many companies outside healthcare have made enormous progress linking their owned sources of value with those they don't own. Healthcare managers do well to look beyond their own industry and examine the connecting strategies of winners like Cisco Systems, Inc.

Who: Cisco Systems, Inc.
How: It uses technology to connect owned and unowned sources of value.

Cisco's business day never ends. Whether the omnipresent company is sending or receiving messages to and from its customers, partners, or suppliers, the Cisco universe sparkles with new ideas and information that constantly zip through cyberspace via the Internet.

Founded in 1984, Cisco is the world leader in creating Internet connecting equipment, both hardware and software. An extraordinary 90 percent of the world's Internet traffic uses its products. More to the point, Cisco itself has become a kind of connecting device — a global network of 34,000 employees who are intricately and intimately linked to customers and suppliers on every continent.

Most of these customers are sizeable organizations that love doing business with Cisco over what has become the world's largest e-commerce site. Ninety percent of Cisco's orders are transacted over its Web site, Cisco Connection Online (CCO), which saves the company nearly $1 billion a year.

Cisco does virtually everything online, connecting its external sources of value, such as its suppliers, to all of its internal processes. One thing it barely does at all any more is make products.

Connectivity began in earnest at Cisco in 1993 when it hired Peter Solvik, the company's pioneering chief information officer. That was also the year that its executive committee realized that more value was added if suppliers, rather than Cisco itself, manufactured the products. The goal became finding a way to have these outside companies build the equipment so that Cisco could concentrate on its own core abilities — corporate strategy, design, engineering, marketing, and customer service.

With Solvik leading the way, Cisco extended its evolving intranet into an extranet that brought its external relationships, including these with suppliers, into a single, highly interdependent enterprise. The outsourcing was reinforced through partnerships with contract equipment manufacturers (CEMs), notably Jabil Circuit, Inc., of St. Petersburg, Florida, and distributors, such as Avnet, Inc., of Great Neck, New York.

Once the extranet linked customers directly to suppliers and partners, Cisco could stop processing orders, managing inventory, and distributing products. Not only did its costs fall by an amazing 30 percent, but the company became more flexible. For example, since it was no longer totally committed to any particular manufacturing process, Cisco could adjust to technological advances by hiring or acquiring whatever other company was on the cutting-edge at the moment.

Initially, Cisco Connection Online handled simple transactions and customer support. Every Cisco department serving customers had been instructed to create its own home page. Though home pages are standard at other online enterprises, this one sparked interdepartmental squabbling that limited the site's effectiveness. In 1996, Solvik took charge, infusing the project with a multitude of artists, designers, and technical writers who transformed the site. Running on Sun Microsystems, Inc. hardware and a Solaris operating system, CCO was

Hospitals, HMOs, and other healthcare organizations, including pharmaceutical companies, are buried in government-regulated, paper-based processes that mire the system in inefficiencies.

able to transcend any one department's parochial interests and become a powerful interface for Cisco's customers.

By 1999, CCO sales had reached $11.7 billion — more than 85 percent of the whole company's revenue. The site saves Cisco $1 billion a year in information-technology expenses, money that the company can roll over into research-and-development investments for better products and services — and for new technologies, open and closed, internal and external, that can be used to connect its owned and unowned assets.

Cisco's success in using technology to link all the elements of its extended enterprise has few parallels in the healthcare industry. According to the Gartner Group, a leading technology-advisory firm, "It's a sad fact that healthcare could benefit greatly from information technology and it hasn't pursued it with enough aggressiveness."

Most hospitals, HMOs, and other healthcare organizations, including large pharmaceutical companies, remain buried in paper-based process-

New technologies offer a powerful and unprecedented means of leveraging all of a company's assets and relationships, tangible and intangible, owned and unowned.

es that mire the system in inefficiencies. We have all experienced the frustration of waiting weeks, even months, for a hospital bill or insurance claim to be settled. In large part, that happens because doctors, insurers, medical facilities, and the government have been reluctant to adopt state-of-the-art technology, systems, and processes to manage their businesses and their customer relationships.

That reluctance can be dangerous in an industry whose errors and omissions may literally kill customers. Indeed, the Food and Drug Administration (FDA) has reportedly withheld approval of some drugs for fear that doctors may lack knowledge about the medications — information that would be easy to retrieve with up-to-date technology.

The *Physician's Desk Reference* (PDR) offers 3,000 pages of detailed instructions in fine print for every drug approved for use in the United States. Yet, this once-a-year volume can hardly keep pace with pharmaceutical progress.

Small wonder that healthcare professionals make mistakes, given the complexity and extraordinary influx of new treatments and drugs. But some of those mistakes could be avoided if medical practitioners received earlier reports on new technologies, delivered at Internet speed.

A case in point is the FDA's recall of the allergy drug Seldane in 1997. Early news reports suggested that Seldane might cause fatal heart problems when taken with the popular antibiotic erythromycin or certain other medications. The FDA's first response was to query doctors about the drug — by letter. Only when actual deaths were attributed to Seldane did the FDA remove it. Imagine how much better and faster that recall would have been had the FDA used email and the Internet rather than letters and phone calls.

Having information is one of the oldest human passions. Driven by curiosity and our appetite for learning, humans have constantly improved the ways we acquire data to the point that technology is considerably ahead of our ability to use it. This is particularly true of a complex industry like healthcare, which is rich in information but poor in communication. Much is known, but not shared, and the common good cries out for ways to connect everyone. The Internet does just that. With its planetary reach, it can democratize and disseminate knowledge on an unprecedented scale. It can flash news to a billion corners of the globe as it actually happens. It can rejuvenate marginal companies and revolutionize whole industries. To make the most of this phenomenal tool is the central challenge of our time.

Connectivity is clearly the key prescription for the healthcare industry. A few pioneers have shown us where and how to go. For example, we began this chapter with WorldCare, Inc., a healthcare organization that relies on technology with excellent results. Intel Corporation is working on the electronic transmission of patient records and other sensitive information in ways that preserve privacy. And WebMD has sought to electronically unify its assets and relationships in order to serve customers, ranging from solo practitioners to global pharmaceutical companies.

Still, connectivity remains a distant goal for most healthcare organizations, the few pioneers notwithstanding. Ironically, the majority's reluctance to catch up with the connected economy stands in sharp contrast with the attitudes of healthcare's key players — its consumers, who are surfing the Web for healthcare information in ever-increasing numbers.

Providing patients with more information is vital but only one aspect of the industry's online potential. According to Forrester Research, Inc.: "The Web will be the foundation for a new healthcare industry infrastructure that can support complex, multi-party transactions among empowered consumers, wired practitioners, real-time supply chains, and service-conscious payers." Forrester predicts that healthcare's business-to-business (B2B) online sales will climb from under $10 billion in 2000 to approximately $350 billion in 2004. By then, B2B will likely comprise one-sixth of overall trade in the healthcare industry.

"To get there," says Forrester, "firms will organize around a healthcare eBusiness network that serves and connects consumers, providers, distribution chains, and payers." The challenge is to ensure that these networks create economic value for all assets and relationships — tangible and intangible, owned and unowned. That outcome is far from automatic. To achieve the success Forrester envisions, healthcare managers must first clearly understand what technologies are needed and why.

Connecting sources of value goes far beyond using technology to transfer existing processes to the Web. It requires re-examining and improving all the relationships that support businesses in today's economy, and doing so within a framework that considers new economic realities holistically. For that to happen, managers must consider their company's customer, supplier, investor, and employee relationships in the context of today's connected economy. They must do so in a total rather than piecemeal manner.

One leader who has achieved that goal is Scott McNealy, chairman and chief executive officer of Sun Microsystems, Inc. He once commented, "The biggest challenge we always have is how to keep investors happy who care about the next four hours, keep customer happy who care about the next year or two, and keep employees happy who want to meet the payroll, and yet build a company that can grow."

In today's business environment, being responsive to one of these markets requires being responsive to them all. Failure to retain talented employees, for example, leads to a decline in customer satisfaction, which leads to a fall in revenue, which will affect stock performance. Supply-chain failures precipitate a similar cycle.

To connect your sources of value, you begin by identifying them and then connecting them via information technology, systems, or processes. We suggest two initial steps:

First, determine the methods you already use to connect your sources of value.

Second, map the technologies, systems, and processes that would enable you to link all your sources of value.

This mapping exercise is intended to help you plot both your current and future connection strategies. It also allows

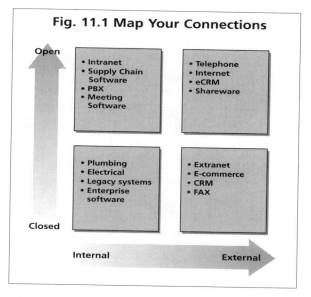

Fig. 11.1 Map Your Connections

you to categorize the sources of value you're connecting more carefully than you may have done before. Along with defining connections as internal or external, for example, you should consider the degree to which you want the connecting technology, system, or process available (open or closed) to others. These two sets of variables (see Figure 11.1) are essential to planning in this area.

For example, an online system for keeping track of your company's finances should obviously be internal and closed to preserve privacy.

Accordingly, you would probably want to install your own wires and use your own servers.

The same may apply when you use enterprise resource-planning (ERP) software, which is highly customized to each individual organization. On the other hand, if you are a pharmaceutical company and considered your suppliers to be partners, you might want them involved in a system that facilitates planning and online testing of new drugs. In that case, the connecting ERP software would be closed but external.

Let's look at how a few healthcare companies connect their sources of value, both internally and across corporate and industry boundaries.

Who: Kaiser Permanente and MedUnite.

How: Each uses technology to connect with customers.

Kaiser Permanente allows members to ask questions and schedule doctor's appointments online. Blue Shield of California is planning to use the Internet to connect its 50,000 doctors and its 2 million plan members.

Six of the biggest U.S. health insurers have jointly launched a Web site called MedUnite, where patients can shop for medical plans, doctors, and hospitals. The consortium aims to improve relationships with doctors by improving communication and reducing business costs.

The online system will also manage administrative services, such as approving or denying medical procedures and processing payment claims. Members of the consortium are Aetna U.S. Healthcare, Cigna Corporation, WellPoint Health Systems, Foundation Health Systems, and PacifiCare Health Systems.

Who: Neoforma.com, Inc. and e-MedSoft.com.

How: Each uses the Internet to connect with suppliers.

Today's healthcare supply chain is not much better than yesterday's. According to U.S. Bancorp, Piper Jaffray's report on eHealth B2B, the current loss from purchasing errors in the healthcare industry has reached $11 billion per year, a waste that begs for the remedial power of digital technology. Nowhere will the Internet be more helpful. It can and must be used to transform the healthcare supply chain.

Five of the nation's largest healthcare distributors have joined in creating an independent online company that will provide information about healthcare products, ranging from bandages to blood plasma and MRIs. The new company is backed by AmeriSource Health Corporation, Cardinal Health, Inc., Fisher Scientific International, McKesson HBOC, and Owens & Minor. It will assist group purchasers and provider organizations to acquire every imaginable medical product. It will also give providers immediate access to information about product availability, contract pricing, and delivery.

Neoforma.com, founded in 1996, has created an electronic bazaar served by approximately 550 suppliers offering an estimated 112,000 stock-keeping units (SKUs). The site also offers hospital designers virtual tours of 1,200 "best-practice" rooms. By clicking on various parts of a virtual room, the user can rotate it, get the price of a piece of equipment, and other information, and obtain a complete bill of materials for every item. The value of such technology is self-evident.

Neoforma.com's medical equipment site offers hospital designers virtual tours of 1,200 "best-practice" rooms. By clicking on various parts of a virtual room, the user can rotate it, get the cost of a piece of equipment, and other information, and obtain a complete bill of materials for every item.

E-MedSoft.com is another of the growing number of companies that enable and improve business processes, while also providing a range of solutions for physicians and managed-care organizations. A newly acquired image-transmission technology, for example, allows physicians and researchers to view, manipulate, store, and analyze tissue data both remotely and locally through a Web-based platform. The new technology is being used at Memorial Sloan Kettering Cancer Center, the University of Maryland, and other academic and commercial institutions.

Who: University Medical Associates (UMA) and MacGregor Medical Association.
How: Each uses technology to improve all of its sources of value.

E-Business solutions can work well for managing work flow across distant locations. Consider the partnership between IBM, based in New York, and Infinium Software, Inc., based in Hyannis, Massachusetts. The two companies were asked to create an e-business solution that would monitor and manage employees working for staff orthopedists at University Medical Associates (UMA), one of the oldest and largest healthcare providers in the southern United States. The physicians' group is affiliated with the Medical University of South Carolina.

UMA encompasses more than 2,200 doctors, nurses, medics, and administrators at several locations. Its human resource managers were struggling with how to manage these highly skilled employees most effectively. Within eight weeks, IBM and Infinium designed a solution that enabled UMA's human resources personnel to manage the company's entire staff as one cohesive unit. The system's remote time-card entry facilitates accurate tracking and analysis of employees. The system gives UMA a unique scheduling tactic: It can match patients' needs with the staff person whose skills are most relevant to those needs. UMA believes that the ability to maximize human resources can dramatically boost productivity and, ultimately, value creation.

Another example is the MacGregor Medical Association, which has 13 satellite facilities in Houston and San Antonio, Texas. To transfer records of its 300,000 patients, MacGregor had used couriers to physically carry the records among the centers. Technology solved that problem. The company developed proprietary software that allows doctors to have their patients' medical histories — diagnoses, medical procedures, immunizations, and drug allergies, dating back to 1991 — online and at their fingertips.

Now, doctors access the records they need on personal computers in their offices, outside examination rooms, at nurses' stations, emergency and delivery rooms of MacGregor-affiliated hospitals, or at home on their computers. The results: better use of valuable professional time and far better medical care.

New technologies, systems, and processes — open and closed, external and internal — that link your company and its assets and relationships cannot guarantee success or improvements in the quality of care. But healthcare organizations that ignore these new technologies, systems, and processes reduce their chances of connecting with their markets and diminish their prospects for improving their performances and profitability.

What does the future look like as buyers, sellers, providers, lenders, and stakeholders in the healthcare industry start to take advantage of connectivity? Donald Berwick, M.D., president of the Boston-based, not-for-profit Institute for Healthcare Improvement, suggests that the industry's "core process" will move from the "provision of a personal service to the provision of information."

Over the next two decades, Berwick maintains, medicine will essentially become a "knowledge producing," not a "contact producing" enterprise. "It is a fundamental reframing of our work, though not of our goals and values." Producing and distributing knowledge is crucial to patient care. Obviously, expensive diagnostic tests have no purpose if their results are not disclosed to the patient. People's health is at stake.

Dr. Berwick argues that when patients need quick information or a medication refill, they do not need appointments with physicians. He points out that "confusing care with [physical] encounters reduces the value of both." Innovative "doctors are using e-mail with patients to become virtually available, even if nobody pays them for it yet. It is only a matter of time before we will all do that and can make a living at it."

By the same token, B2B exchanges are beginning, in the words of Piper Jaffray analysts, to help "move the health supply chain to the 'Holy Grail' of having the right product in the right place at the right time in an efficient manner." They continue: "Efforts to work collaboratively in both healthcare and other industries are beginning to emerge. But the reality is that the best way to improve the supply chain is not to cut budgets and expenditures, but rather to invest in new technologies that will help redefine the fundamental way organizations do business." And that means making all kinds of data easily accessible. If patients can deteriorate, even die, because they can't or don't know how to procure information on treating their diseases, the same is true for companies. Organizations that do not have an efficient system for disclosing and disseminating research results, just to name one type of information, will be unable to function.

▶ What's Next?

 We have argued that intangible assets and relationships, owned or not, are more important than ever before in providing for healthcare's future. In this chapter, we have introduced the concept of using technology to connect and maximize the assets and relationships that matter today. Until your company makes those connections, we argue, it cannot fully realize the potential of its business model and its diverse sources of value.

Still ahead of us looms a significant challenge — measurement. To properly manage and make the most of their sources of value, companies must be able to measure them correctly. We consider it a given that you can only manage well what you can measure accurately.

Our ability to measure tangible assets is fairly well understood. But such is not the case with intangibles and relationships. The tools we have today for that task are limited. We must develop new ways to measure all sources of value and report it to stakeholders, and this is the subject of the next chapter.

Questions to ask yourself.

Business Model: We have seen how different businesses use different technologies to connect their sources of value both internally and externally. How does your own business compare? Is your company's business model based primarily on using your own assets, relationships, and internal technologies, or are you using today's technologies to connect with your suppliers, partners, and customers?

Risk: As we discussed in the previous chapter, risks emerge from the relationships you don't have and the technologies you don't use as well as from those that you do. What risk-management tools and techniques have you put in place to monitor these elements to insure that your business model survives and thrives?

Technology: Does your company use technology, systems, and processes to their fullest potential? Or does it use them only to protect its entrenched way of doing business? In other words, do you use technology simply to speed up the pace and cut down the cost of maintaining the status quo? If so, you could be headed for trouble.

Measurement: Do you have a clear understanding of your resources? Do they enable you to fully measure all the assets in your company's portfolio, including their interconnections? Can you measure the effects of using your connected assets to maximum competitive advantage? Can your measurements tell you which assets and relationships are the most valuable? Hard questions — but the next chapter is full of the measured answers you need to ensure success.

12 MEASURE AND MANAGE ALL YOUR SOURCES OF VALUE.

Complete and accurate information compiled by reliable sources should be available in real time to all appropriate people, especially stakeholders, whether they are within or outside of the organization.

During the fall of 2000, the Securities and Exchange Commission (SEC) moved aggressively to level the playing field for investors.

To the delight of most stock buyers, the SEC approved the much-debated Regulation Fair Disclosure, now widely called Reg FD. The new regulation is designed to provide everyone — institutional and retail investors alike — with equal access to important, market-moving information from all public companies, regardless of the industry.

What does Reg FD mean to your healthcare corporation? Whether your enterprise is private or public, Reg FD portends the beginning of a major change in what financial information you must report to whom and how. The new standard is "fair disclosure," a giant step in the right direction.

Full disclosure is, of course, something else. Feared by those who thrive on secrecy, welcomed by those who see openness as a business strength, full disclosure awaits the day when managers perceive its actual benefit to the bottom line.

Yet value depends enormously on measurement, which, in turn, is profoundly important to how you create prosperity no matter what business you're in. You can neither run a business effectively, nor make thoughtful decisions without reliable measurement and management systems.

Even so, most companies remain unable to see today's most important sources of value, which means they neither measure nor manage them effectively. Our research, which involves more than 10,000 actively traded companies in U.S. markets, offers evidence on this point. Between 1978 and 2000, book assets declined from 95 to 24 percent of total market value. In other words, investors began measuring companies in terms of sources of value that the companies themselves did not carry on their balance sheets and presumably did not recognize as valuable. Accordingly, the above numbers mean that 76 percent (more than three-quarters) of the value of all public companies is not accounted for as assets at fair value in our current measurement systems.

Companies will need to continuously measure and report all sources of value at fair value to all users.

In short, our research suggests that incomplete performance measurement creates faulty economic decisions. Why have most attempts to resuscitate many healthcare organizations been wasted on short-term, circular efforts? One answer, though not the only one, is that our current measurement system too often misinforms and misguides healthcare and business leaders. Research shows, for example, that leaders may misinterpret measurement results and think that cutting medical and administrative staff is a useful way to control expenses, which, in fact may eliminate the very people and knowledge that every organization needs to rejuvenate itself.

In short, your own healthcare company's measurement system is probably not generating all the information you and your investors need to guide your operating and capital-budgeting decisions. The situation is worse in the not-for-profit sector, which lacks investors who might demand accurate measures.

Now: Assets are measured, in part, at book value and only periodically.
Next: All sources of value are measured, at fair value, and reported in real time to all stakeholders.

Current measurement practices can be summed up as a company's sporadic and cursory review of what a few of its assets and none of its important relationships cost. As more and more companies feel the effects of not having reliable information, what are now considered appropriate measurement systems will be deemed inadequate and insufficient. Indeed, we have no hesitation in prophesying a transformation in the way healthcare companies measure and thus manage the assets so critical to their prosperity. Sooner rather than later we believe our prophecy will be proven correct: *Companies will need to continuously measure and report all sources of value at fair value to all users.*

Our prophecy will constitute a value revolution for your entire healthcare company and its stakeholders. This assumes, of course, that you see the future early and get aboard before it passes you by.

Bear in mind, inaccurate or incomplete information leads to bad decisions. Volatility emerges from sources of value that are neither measured nor properly managed. Yet such confusion is avoidable. There is only one reason for it to befall your organization — it will happen if you let it happen. And you won't: Not after seeing the benefits that good measure can bring to your company. And definitely not after reaping the profits derived from managing those well-measured assets and relationships.

How can your healthcare company master this transformation? Remember our story about Tony L. White, the leader profiled in Chapter 3. White took the job as chief executive at Perkin-Elmer (now called Applera), a lagging medical equipment manufacturer, after he spotted a few promising assets. One was the rights to the polymerase chain reaction, or PCR, a chemical process for copying DNA, and the other was Applied Biosystems, Inc., a manufacturer of DNA sequencers that used PCR.

White had a vision of how to turn these two unmeasured and unreported sources of value into an enormous success, and he successfully

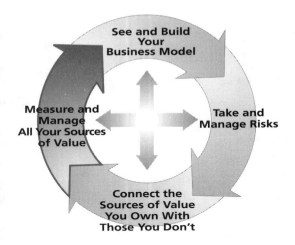

See and Build Your Business Model

Measure and Manage All Your Sources of Value

Take and Manage Risks

Connect the Sources of Value You Own With Those You Don't

acted upon it. Today, the company is comprised of two business units with separate tracking stocks: Applied Biosystems and Celera Genomics Group. Applied Biosystems, the manufacturing unit, builds the world's fastest DNA gene sequencers, as well as systems for AIDS research and forensic medicine. Celera Genomics was formed in 1998 to sequence the human genome, which it has successfully completed.

For White and his investors, the lesson was inescapable. Had they relied on conventional performance measurement, they would have missed the opportunity to document the human genome and reap tremendous rewards in the process. They saw what others did not. As the great French scientist Louis Pasteur said, "Chance favors the prepared mind."

Can your company spot opportunities like White's? Pasteur's open-mindedness would certainly help. Beyond attitude, the first practical step is to adopt measurement methodologies and performance indicators that can help you value all your company's sources of value. The second step is to begin to share this information with all your stakeholders in real time. Your company needs to join the Information Economy, where the data required for effective decision-making are becoming more transparent and available round the clock.

How do you value assets and relationships that traditional measurement systems never valued before? For assets that have quantifiable worth outside your business — customers, suppliers, and independent contractors, for instance — you can simply use fair value. Intangible assets, such as proprietary knowledge or brands, are obviously harder to value. To begin with, any source of value must be transferable between sellers and buyers in order to establish its fair value. But right now, the markets for transferable, intangible assets and relationships are immature, compared with those for financial and fixed assets. Information about intangible assets is often scarce. As a result, their prices and exchange rates are elusive and may be available only from disparate sources. In some instances, your decisions will rely on subjective and qualitative information.

This will change. New sources of quantified data are emerging as companies become more familiar with the panoply of factors that contribute to market value. Meanwhile, there are other sources of information about assets. Trading on the stock markets produces a huge statistical base detailing a company's financial performance. Purchases by customers generate information about consumer markets. People in the labor market create information about employment. Government requirements draw forth proxies and other invaluable data. Organizations in the service sector, for example, tend to focus on employees — the service deliverers, as it were. Organizations on the retail side prefer to allocate more support to their customers, seeking, for instance, to mine information from customer questionnaires. With the advent of digital exchanges and auctions, the pricing and trading of these sources of value will be easier and more common. We believe that markets will emerge around all these sources of value, just like in the financial markets today.

By "markets" we mean far more than financial or wholesale markets, now the most familiar kinds.

Consider the rapid emergence of exchanges for intellectual property. Pl-x.com has established The Patent & License Exchange, Inc., which is a marketplace for the sale of rated, insured, and independently priced intellectual property. Meanwhile, Intellectual Property Technology Exchange, Inc., has established TechEx, an Internet-based,

Your company needs to be part of the Information Age, where data is becoming more transparent and available 24 by 7.

business-to-business exchange. TechEx links technologies from research laboratories to licensing professionals in life science companies. At patentauction.com, you can purchase or license various forms of intellectual property, including patents, patent applications, technological know-how, trade secrets, copyrights, and trademarks. And BTG plc, a British government research body that was privatized in 1992, established a transactional Web site, which offers an estimated 8,500

At patentauction.com, you can purchase or license various forms of intellectual property, including patents, patent applications, technological know-how, trade secrets, copyrights, and trademarks.

patents in communication, semiconductors, integrated media, security and ID, and biomedical fields.

Such new information-based enterprises are appearing at a rapid pace. Access to them is being improved by new market makers and "infomediaries," many of them online. Soon it will be much easier to estimate the fair value of all sources of value, including your company's intangibles.

But that's only part of the story. The measurement issue has another aspect — how and how well information gets gathered and stored in the first place. Business information affects all of us and determines numerous types of transactions — which products customers buy, which stocks investors sell, and which companies employees decide to work for are just a few examples. Most important is that performance reporting shapes every company's investments in assets and relationships.

Thus reliable information is critical not only to the healthcare industry, but to our overall economy. Without well-informed capital allocation, we can't hope to promote productivity, nurture innovation, and encourage investment in our future. Conversely, flawed capital allocation resulting from incomplete, insufficient information will invite unproductive medical practices and a higher cost of capital.

Even if we create methodologies that measure all sources of value, if we fail to share all that we have learned with our stakeholders, we subvert the decision makers who are charged with assessing the risks and rewards of allocating resources and seizing opportunities. Complete and accurate information compiled from reliable sources should be available in real time to all appropriate people, especially stakeholders, whether they are inside or outside the organization. Only then can you feel confident that everyone concerned with your organization is prepared to commit its scarce resources to the most valuable alternatives.

For company-specific information, your management team needs to be where the buck stops, the ultimate source of reliable information. The team's information must be relevant as well as accurate to meet the needs of three basic audiences:

1 Internal users, who need solid facts to make capital-allocation decisions, such as which projects to fund, which employees to train, and which customers to acquire.

2 Investors and other external users who need accurate information in order to risk their capital by buying your stock or contributing to your fund drive — that is, investments that enhance your growth, but only if the outsiders trust your information and the story you tell.

3 Customers and other external users who rely on your information to help them decide which products and services to buy, which company to work for, or which potential customers to target as buyers of their own products and services.

All in all, the healthcare industry is probably second to none in terms of public hunger for its expertise and the trust it earns when it releases medical information vital to people's lives. In this sense, the industry has unique opportunities to establish customer relationships. Examples:

Who: Medscape, HealthGrades.com, and Medline.
How: Each uses the Internet to connect with its customers.

A number of healthcare companies have set up Web sites to provide customers and potential customers with medical information. Medscape, for instance, offers information on medical trials, and will send patients e-mail notifications of requested material. Denver-based HealthGrades.com has compiled data from a wealth of public and private sources on more than 650,000 physicians, 5,000 hospitals, and 400 health plans. It rates their performances using formulas developed by medical experts and biostatisticians, then offers its results to the public.

The long-time leader in this area is the U.S. government. Medline, the most comprehensive source of professional medical information, is part of the National Institutes of Health's National Library of Medicine. In 1998, the library launched Medlineplus to make medical data more accessible to people outside that profession. Its offerings include online medical encyclopedias and dictionaries to help site visitors interpret medical language. In addition, the NIH has established ClinicalTrials.gov with information on more than 4,000 federal and private medical studies conducted at more than 47,000 locations nationwide.

Thus far, consumers are welcoming these offerings with open arms, but they want to see them expanded to include other aspects of healthcare. Cyber Dialogue reports that 78 percent of consumers would like their health insurers to be online and 37 percent are willing to switch carriers to gain that capability.

Given their head start sharing medical information, healthcare organizations have an opportunity to enhance their reputations even more by sharing their business information. Imagine the potential effect of, say, a great hospital upgrading its financial documentation to a level approximating the accuracy and authority of its medical documentation. For one thing, the result would do wonders for the hospital in the investment community and, presumably, lead to better capital allocation. That, in turn, would surely benefit the hospitals' patients and providers. Moreover, it would behoove healthcare organizations to make use of the online information technologies that are revolutionzing other industries.

When you think about it, few things are as important to healthcare's future as the effective allocation of capital, and that process is dependent on business information. Here's our three-step prescription for success (to learn more about valuation techniques beyond the scope of this chapter, see the end notes):

❶ Assess your current measurement and reporting with a 2-by-2 matrix (Figure 12.1) indicating where you stand. On the vertical axis, the range is from periodic reporting to real-time measurement. On the horizontal, it goes from internal to external. The idea is to characterize your measurement. Possible combinations include internal and periodic, internal and real-time, external and periodic, external and real-time.

❷ Share all non-financial measures internally. To complete that step, you need key performance indicators for all sources of value, which will influence your daily decisions, just as financial information does. With this data, you will be able to fund the most valuable business opportunities thus insuring that your organization is well on its way towards creating and managing its value revolution.

❸ Begin to report in real time, first internally, but ultimately externally, the performance of all your sources of value at their fair value to all stakeholders. With this information, your company and its investors can properly allocate their scarce resources to your company as well as to others in your industry. In so doing, they will be able to price their capital — labor, investments, and purchase power — properly.

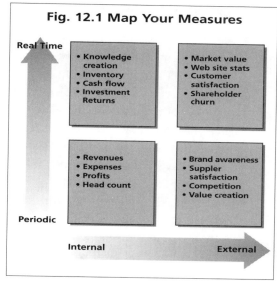

Fig. 12.1 Map Your Measures

Real Time

- Knowledge creation
- Inventory
- Cash flow
- Investment Returns

- Market value
- Web site stats
- Customer satisfaction
- Shareholder churn

- Revenues
- Expenses
- Profits
- Head count

- Brand awareness
- Suppler satisfaction
- Competition
- Value creation

Periodic

Internal   External

Who: Cisco Systems, Inc.
How: Real-time measurement and reporting.

Cisco has linked all its operations, internal and external, so that financial and non-financial data, such as sales, product margins, customer satisfaction, and employee productivity are visible in real time. That capacity to measure and report makes it possible for the company to close its books on an hour's notice. In other words, Cisco's continuous and transparent information reveals problems and opportunities as they occur.

Our point is that no company is immune from the repercussions of having inadequate and inaccurate information with which to make decisions. No business should wait for regulators to make it aware of its need to obtain information that will support value creation.

▶ What's Next?

As we have discussed, intense competition and rapid advances in technology have imposed entirely new business conditions throughout healthcare and other industries. In response, successful healthcare enterprises are transforming how they are organized and managed, how they develop new products and services, how they assume risks and nurture relationships, both inside and outside their boundaries. In sum, they are changing everything.

In today's volatile economy, the winners in every industry focus on reviewing and improving all their relationships. They discard internal and external processes that add little value. They decentralize decision making. They provide information to more people who perform key activities. They develop new relationships with suppliers, employees, and customers — even with their competitors. The result: soaring productivity and far greater value.

To those ends, companies are changing their information systems as well as the types of information they use and share to manage their businesses. This enables their investors and bondholders to make smarter decisions. For example, some companies are developing new financial and non-financial performance measures that include previously unreported and unrecorded statistics, such as employee productivity, customer acquisition costs and satisfaction, and supply-chain capacity.

Where does all this leave your company? Surely it needn't be vulnerable to the dramatic changes and opportunities affecting business in general and healthcare in particular. The most fruitful and practical response is to hone your company's measurement and management practices. Only when managers have all of the relevant information on their company's value-adding assets and relationships can they enable their businesses to capitalize on rapid change.

Questions to ask yourself.

Business Model: Are you measuring the assets and relationships that create value for your organization? Is sharing information with your stakeholders a natural part of your business model? Don't answer this question yourself. Ask all your stakeholders — investors, customers, employees, and suppliers.

Risk: Incomplete information creates risk. Complete information mitigates it. How transparent is the information in your organization? Who sees it? Who sees through it?

Technology: How are you using technology to gather and share information inside your organization? Are you using technology to gather and share information outside your organization?

Measurement: What sources of value have you traditionally measured in your organization? Have you measured their fair value? Do the companies discussed in this chapter suggest any new measures to you? What do you intend to measure in the next two years? In the next five years?

13

IT'S TIME TO MANAGE WHAT MATTERS IN HEALTHCARE.

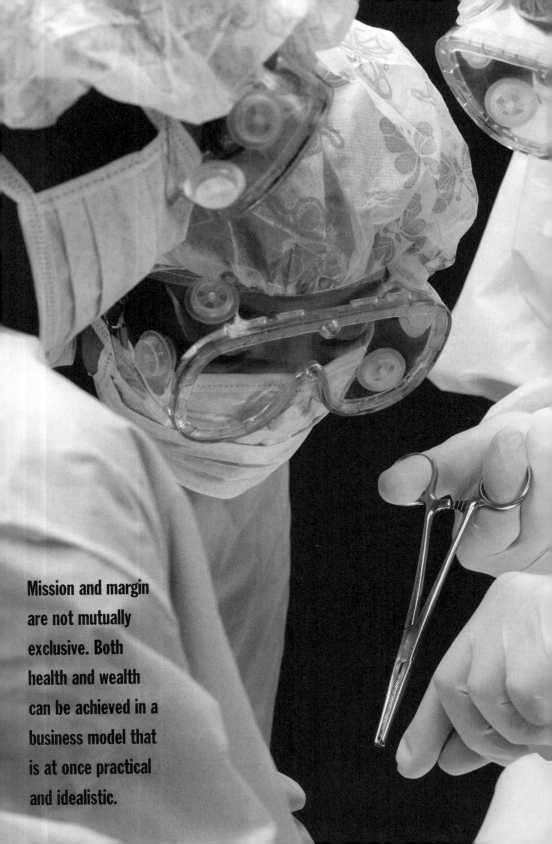

Mission and margin
are not mutually
exclusive. Both
health and wealth
can be achieved in a
business model that
is at once practical
and idealistic.

Because he was the first healer to record his experiences as a physician and a teacher, Hippocrates is known as the Father of Medicine.

But before he would share his considerable medical knowledge and skills with a student, Hippocrates required the novice to take an oath. Twenty-four centuries later, that oath remains honored by generation after generation of physicians as the ethical standard for the practice of medicine.

The oath requires that doctors follow a regimen "for the benefit of my patients" and abstain "from whatever is deleterious and mischievous. . . . With purity and with holiness I will pass my life and practice my art."

Like any other commitment to an ideal, people have often violated the Hippocratic Oath. Yet, the spirit of the oath endures, both in patients' faith and expectations, and in the actual workings of the entire healthcare industry. Indeed, it is a measure of the power of this idea that it is universally accepted as the way things ought to be. Not only the physicians who take the oath, but nurses and other healthcare professionals are committed to preserving human life. Hospital administrators work to provide quality services that are supported by state-of-the-art medical equipment and technologies. A host of care providers, from ambulance drivers and laboratory technicians to X-ray processors and physical therapists, spend their working lives keeping people healthy. Biotechnology and pharmaceutical companies race to discover new treatments for disease.

Some medical professionals, however, believe that the contemporary healthcare industry has strayed too far from Hippocrates' standards. In protest, they created a "Call to Action," signed by thousand of doctors and nurses and published in the *Journal of the American Medical Association* in 1997. They wrote: "Canons of commerce are displacing dictates of healing, trampling our profession's most sacred values." One of the 99 theses in the article stated that the "pursuit of corporate profit and personal fortune has no place in care-giving."

These critics are misguided; they fail to understand the history of their own profession. They seem to believe that commercial success and value creation for those who deliver healthcare are in some way unethical and detrimental to the precepts of the Hippocratic Oath. In our view, of course, nothing could be further from the truth.

In reality, commerce has marched in step with healthcare since the very beginning of medical practice. Even Hippocrates demanded that each of his students swear to "reckon him who taught me this art equally dear to me as my parents, to share my substance with him, and to relieve his necessities if required; to look upon his offspring in the same footing." Clearly, Hippocrates' voluntarily placed himself amidst an economic enterprise.

Patients have historically viewed healthcare much more as a profession of sacrifice and dedication than a business of value creation. They feel doctors and nurses were motivated to help others and will act from the heart rather than the pocketbook. That expectation continues and carries over to hospitals, ambulance services, medical equipment makers, and even pharmaceutical manufacturers. When healthcare companies and individuals profit, people may suspect that it comes at the expense of patients. The public's idealized physician is not the Lexus-driving cardiac specialist, but the valise-toting old-time family doctor making house calls on snowy evenings — or perhaps the dedicated slum doctor of Gerald Green's best-seller, *The Last Angry Man.*

This characterization is neither accurate nor reasonable. Yes, professionals and managers in healthcare acknowledge their special ethical obligations, but this does not oblige them to be selfless. Providing and receiving healthcare is like any economic exchange in which money changes hands and it operates by the same rules.

These markets are the proper study of healthcare managers. In labor, capital, product, service, and other markets, managers can learn what creates and destroys value. Our message to patients as well as to healthcare practitioners and managers, is this: Markets are to be respected and learned from, not to be feared.

In this final chapter, we consider the issue of mission versus margin. We also present our own call to action for the entire healthcare industry.

We hold that value creation in healthcare is not only ethical — it is essential. What's more, it is two-sided. The value created for patients is good health, and if practitioners and investors who provide that did

Markets are to be respected and learned from, not to be feared.

not get economic value in return, medicine would still be in the dark ages. The ability to earn a profit for stakeholders by developing important products and services is what drives value creation in any industry, and healthcare is no exception. And, as in any other industry, the wish for gain is also a powerful incentive for caregivers to deliver products and services efficiently and effectively. Without the possibility of profit, the healthcare industry as we know it would disappear, along with any further advances in medical technology, intellectual property, and medical research.

The Hippocratic Oath reflects a basic connection between doing well and doing good. Its taboo on "deleterious and mischievous" behavior expresses a fundamental principle of value creation in any industry: That value is created only in a voluntary exchange in which all parties benefit means that wealth transferred through any other means, including erroneous information, does not create value. Thus, it is the advantage of all industries to avoid business dealings that do not benefit every-one involved.

Like the Hippocratic Oath, that principle is an expression of an ideal. But what happens if the exchange is not wholly voluntary? The health-care industry is very complex, in part because consumers do not pay for their services directly, but are "protected" from having to negotiate fees. Since managed-care companies and government agencies control the cost of healthcare delivery by contracting with providers, the prices that the market might dictate are smothered beneath Medicare subsidies and HMO contracts. Patients with insurance rarely even ask what their care will cost. Hospitals are at constant war with HMOs and insurance adjusters over what procedures and practices are billable. Other health-care professionals — doctors, nurses, X-ray technicians, therapists, pharmacists, and lab technicians — also struggle under these con-straints.

Barriers to communication in the industry also inhibit collaboration among healthcare practitioners in different disciplines and hinder the cooperative exchange of information among practitioners and man-agers. Hospital administrators and staffers are caught between, on the one hand, the conflicting demands of patients, caregivers, the HMOs, and insurance companies that administer payments, and, on the other, the employers whose money is at stake. The possibility of litigation cre-ates another barrier to communication and fosters treatment and diag-nostic tests that are not needed.

As we have seen, advances in business and information technology, like the electronic medical record (EMR), are breaking through these bar-riers. Eventually, EMR will revolutionize the exchange of business infor-mation, forging real-time links among doctors, hospitals, payers, labora-tories, pharmacies, and patients, within one organization or across many. Indeed, eventually everyone will have a health card that provides him or her instant access to his/her medical record via the Internet.

The Internet, too, is educating patients and, in many ways, is doing a poor job. While physicians have learned to dread patients who are primed with wrong information procured from chatrooms, legitimate medical sources have helped millions to understand their ailments and cooperate with the cures.

Despite promising developments, the healthcare industry's current issues are clearly reflected in the uneven way its sectors are rewarded. Physicians complain loudly that their practices are being disrupted by the demands of HMOs, insurers, and the threat of litigation. HMOs and insurers complain that physicians are calling for unnecessary and costly diagnostic testing. Pharmaceutical companies complain that their profits are being undermined by generic drugs. Hospitals complain that soaring expenses and other price pressures make it almost impossible to raise funds in the bond market.

Without the possibility of profit, the healthcare industry as we know it would disappear, along with any further advances in medical technology, intellectual property, and medical research.

At the same time, however, enormous value is being created in some healthcare areas, including the pharmaceutical, medical-equipment, and biotechnology sectors. How is this discrepancy, this gap in value creation, possible? It derives from the failure of much of the industry to thoroughly understand and dedicate itself to the real principles of value creation. Mission and margin are not mutually exclusive. Both health and wealth can be achieved in a business model that is at once practical and idealistic. In the end, every healthcare organization will benefit from understanding that it is a business made up of assets and relationships through which it realizes its unique mission. When healthcare recognizes that its business models are based on these sources of value, the industry can be healthy again — and that, in turn, will enhance the health, wealth, and quality of life of individuals, families, and our entire society. This book has been a journey to that conclusion.

A Paradox of Value.

It will not be easy to break free of the old models and adopt new ones. As we have seen, a great deal of history, policy, and habituation obstructs the path.

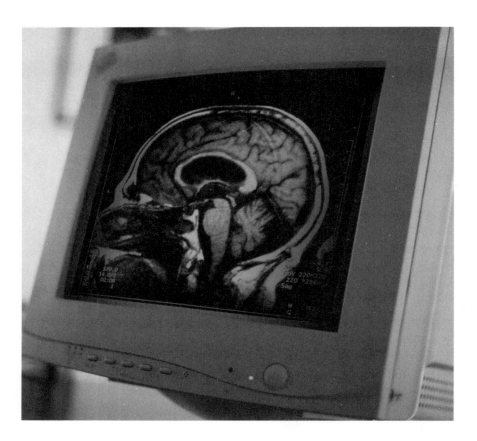

To begin with, the healthcare industry's traditional measurement system drives managers to measure their success by outmoded yardsticks. Assets and return on capital are expressed almost entirely in physical and financial terms, and this can lead to decisions that are based on incomplete information. In an industry that is driven by service and information, managers find that they must think and act like widget makers, valuing bricks and mortar ahead of talent, customers, suppliers, and even research and development.

It is no consolation that a significant portion of the industry is not subject to the discipline of the markets. Too many not-for-profit organizations continue to operate under the assumption that the measures of business success and accountability that apply to their for-profit colleagues are irrelevant to their own operations. This is untrue — not-for-profits must make a profit if they are to survive.

Because these organizations live by different standards, they rarely tap the equity markets, thereby drastically limiting their access to capital. We presume that an inescapable rule of organizational life is that institutions not governed by investors lack the continuing pressure to create value that is so essential in today's economy.

A large sector of the industry falls under government regulation, which entails its own paradoxes. Managers must be prepared for abrupt declines in reimbursement levels when government budgets are cut, but must still contrive to invest in the relationships (such as talented staff and service to patients) that really matter to their success.

The parts of the industry that have been "deregulated" (including insurers, health-management organizations, and care providers whose patients must pay their own bills) are under pressure once again to reduce the cost of care. But in practice, this encourages not the management of care but the management of price, spurring more ICC-informed decisions, physicians' protests, and patients' dissatisfaction. As we pointed out earlier, a similar unrest, bordering on revolt, has overtaken the airline industry. Unless and until healthcare finds better ways of accommodating its customer and employee assets, the lynchpins of business success, the industry will, most likely experience greater strain.

As it stands, the healthcare system has become seriously distorted. Wealth flows to managed care companies, pharmaceutical makers, and selected physicians, while hospitals struggle financially, insurers abandon whole classes of patients, medical costs consist increasingly of paper work, and payroll deductions across the country balloon to pay for it all. Because no one can see, manage, and measure the assets and relationships that really matter, the industry is at once inefficient and ineffective.

From the perspective of medical technology, the U.S. healthcare system is indisputably the best in the world. But, at the same time, it is among the most costly. Its various sectors, may appear to be synergistic, but, in fact, have diverging (and sometimes conflicting) goals and

Cyber Dialogue, a Web site that helps its users find health information, estimates that it had more than 40 million consumers online in the second quarter of 2000.

incentives. They cannot work together to create real value for themselves, the patients, or society as a whole.

Often, we hear critics of the U.S. healthcare industry hail one or another healthcare experiment abroad. But the economic and social differences between the United States and other nations make most of their experiments irrelevant. As this book makes clear, we believe the appropriate, practical model for healthcare is to be found right here, in the experience of successful companies and industries both within and outside of healthcare proper.

Inevitably, in the long run, our healthcare industry will change. As the aging baby-boom generation increases its demands on the system, institutions will be forced to respond, and the convergence of information technology and biotechnology will radically alter the delivery of healthcare. But inevitable is not the same as timely, and change is not the same as improvement. If the industry fails to learn how to create real value, tomorrow's system may be just as problematic as today's.

To avoid this and create a truly synergistic system, let us repeat our rules for success:

 ❶ In the course of making strategic, operational and financial decisions, keep all the sources of value firmly in mind.

❷ Behavior must change throughout your organization to bring your new business model to life. And that requires you to align your investment and operating strategies with your business model. Creating value is all about taking risks, which requires you to change what you do and how you do it.

❸ Use today's technologies to connect assets and relationships seamlessly, translating that integration into competitive advantage. This will enable you to develop new and innovative relationships with customers, suppliers, investors, employees, and communities.

❹ You cannot manage what you do not measure. Every company must measure its sources of value. But that is not enough. You must communicate your new measures. In addition to your employees and investors, Wall Street analysts, and public-policy regulators, among others, must be persuaded to measure the organization by what truly matters. Your customers, employees, and other stakeholders are constantly making decisions that affect your company's prospects; managers are responsible for assuring that they receive the needed information to make good decisions.

Of course, you, as a manager working in real time, are in no position to wait for the new formal measurement systems to evolve. You will have to find ways to create value

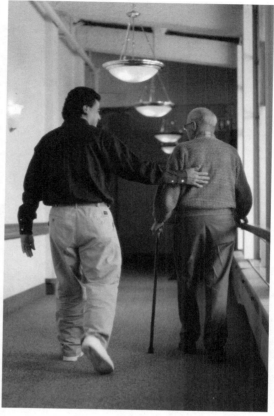

with the new tools we have been describing, while operating within the traditional framework. The goal is to embrace the techniques that already exist for investing in and managing the assets that matter today.

What does all this mean in practical terms for managers in the healthcare industry? In condensed form, we recommend **a call to action—how to make an impact** on value in the healthcare industry—on the following page.

We have come to the end of our journey and this is your call to action as a practitioner or manager in the healthcare industry. You have personally seen and probably experienced the problems and opportunities of your industry. You have surely read and listened to myriad experts with snappy answers and quick fixes for what ails healthcare.

In our view, the solution for the industry is neither simple nor quick. It is basic. But the time to get started on applying that solution is now.

A Call to Action — How to Make an Impact

	Model Concept	Risk	Processes & Technology	Measurement & Reporting
Consumers	Demand better, access to service, faster information, and value (i.e., the best for less and not just low).	Do business with astute risk takers.	Embrace technology.	Demand asset-specific information.
Business Managers and Governance	Embrace change and innovation by investing in the assets that matter.	Take risks like an astute investor.	Use new technologies to link all internal and external sources of value or value sources.	Create new performance measures for all assets.
Investors	Invest in value creating enterprises.	Reward astute investors who take risks.	Reward companies that invest in new technologies and next practices.	Redefine the credit-rating system to accommodate all the assets and relationships that matter.
Regulators/ Public Policy Makers	Eliminate barriers to value creation.	Enable risk-taking.	Reimburse investment in the assets, relationships, and technologies that create value.	Establish performance measures for the assets that create value.

You may recall that we began this book with a discussion of the conquest of the human genome by the two teams, one governmental, the other a private business called Celera Genomics. At Celera, this message appeared on the company's Web site: "Discoveries can't wait." We would suggest you put a sign on your desk that reads, "Value creation can't wait."

What we propose here is practical, realistic, and consistent with the moral standards of healthcare. It calls upon managers and practitioners to continue in the tradition of the Hippocratic Oath, acting in the interest of patients, while shunning "whatever is deleterious and mischievous."

Throughout history, the larger mission of healthcare practitioners and managers has been to create value, for both themselves and their patients. That is what has made healthcare the most elevated of businesses. Today, the manifest changes in the economy require that you learn a new and expanded definition of economic value, and apply it to meet the current and future needs of your company and its stakeholders. In that way, you can help to return the industry to health, creating the value that can, more than anything else, assure the realization of its mission.

EPILOGUE

Inspired by two unlikely allies — DNA science and professional accounting — this book argues that all industries, especially healthcare, now confront the most golden of opportunities. By adopting genetics as a guiding metaphor, companies can vastly multiply the value of their assets relationships, dramatically leverage their investments, and nearly guarantee their success in today's economy.

Scientists have shown that human life derives from the genetic code, nature's instruction book for assembling a healthy person. The code includes 30,000 genes, far less than originally estimated, that transmit characteristics from generation to generation. Good health depends on the proper interaction of those molecules.

Scientists have lately begun to pinpoint errant genes — the ones that cause hereditary defects and diseases like Alzheimer's. The next step is gene therapy: the exciting work of using normal genes to replace defective genes, or to bolster immunity to disease.

We view every organization's sources of value as analogous to human genes. In business, companies combine their assets and relationships in infinite ways to create value in ways that are unique to each company. But value can be mutated by injurious forces, ranging from bad strategy to the total neglect of the assets and relationships that are the key sources of wealth today.

We believe that all businesses, and healthcare in particular, are vulnerable to value mutation, largely caused by outdated measurement and management systems that fail to consider a company's true worth, leaving its managers blind to its possibilities.

If value mutation needlessly destroys an organization's worth, the solution, we argue, lies in asset and relationship therapy — the use of new measurement and management techniques that allow business managers to see all sources of value fully and fairly. We believe the changes we advocate can transform thousands of companies, enabling managers to begin using what most never knew they possessed — a full set of assets and relationships.

We believe these changes are essential for business success — and that every manager can and must adopt them.

That is our Rx for value.

SOURCES

Chapter One

Source for the quote from Francis Crick: Brian Hayes, "Computing Science, The Invention of the Genetic Code," *American Scientist*, January-February 1998.

Sources for the Human Genome information include: Matt Ridley, *Genome* (HarperCollins Publishers, Inc. 1999), p. 5; David Stipp, "Blessings From The Book Of Life," *Fortune*, March 6, 2000, p. F21; www.pe-corp.com.

Source for the quote from Charles Handy, author of *The Hungry Spirit*: Charles Handy, *The Hungry Spirit*, (Broadway Books, 1999).

Sources for the healthcare statistics include: Deanna Bellandi, "Making Money but Struggling," *Modern Healthcare*, August 30, 1999; "Is the Sky Falling?" *Cain Brothers*, March, 2000; "Healthcare Industry Credit Downgrades to Continue," *Healthcare Financial Management*, March, 2000; www.hfma.org.

Source for the quote from Raymond V. Gilmartin, chairman, president and chief executive officer, Merck & Company, Inc.: Raymond V. Gilmartin, "Leadership Roles in Society," Speech, delivered to the American Medical Association 1999 National Leadership Development Conference, March 21, 1999.

Source for the quote from Ron Wolf, executive vice president and general manager, Green Bay Packers: Lucy McCauley, "How Do You Measure Success?" *National Post*, May 8, 1999, p. D12.

Chapter Two

Source for the German proverb: Jerry Mayer and John P. Holms, *Bite-Size Einstein* (New York: St. Martins Press, 1996), p. 31.

Source for the quote from Robert Reich, former U.S. Labor Secretary: Carole Buia, "Your Bagel Or Your Job," *Time*, February 12, 2001, p. 68.

Source for the Medtronic, Inc., information: Tim Stevens, "Heart & Soul," *Industry Week*, May 4, 1998, p. 44.

Source for the quote from Michael S. Malone, editor, *Forbes ASAP*: Michael S. Malone, "Digital Age Values," *Forbes ASAP*, April 3, 2000.

Source for the quote from Paul Hawken: Paul Hawken, *The Ecology of Commerce* (New York: HarperCollins Publishers, Inc., 1994).

Source for the quote from John T. Chambers, chief executive officer of Cisco Systems, Inc.: John A. Byrne, "Visionary vs. Visionary," *Business Week*, August 21-28, 2000, p. 210.

Source for the quote from Hedrick Smith, Pulitzer Prize-winning journalist: Olivia Barker, "Health Care Systems Gets 'Critical' Diagnosis," *USA Today*, October 16, 2000.

Source for the Microsoft Network (MSN) information: www.microsoft.com.

Source for the U.S. Institute for Medicine information: www.nationalacademies.org.

Source for the Japanese government information: Peter Landers, "Japanese Balance Sheet Raises Tough Questions," *The Asian Wall Street Journal*, October 11, 2000, p. 1.

Source for the quote from Arthur Levin, consumer-health advocate: Olivia Barker, "Health Care Systems Gets 'Critical' Diagnosis," *USA Today*, October 16, 2000.

Chapter Three

Source for the quote from Captain D. Michael Abrashoff, U.S. Navy: Polly LaBarre, "The Agenda – Grassroots Leadership," *Fast Company*, April 1999, p. 114.

Sources for the Applera Corporation information include: Julie Bell, "Man Behind Genome Map. Leader," *The Baltimore Sun*, July 30, 2000, p. D1; Andrew Pollack, "The Microsoft (and Gates) of the Genome Industry," *The New York Times*, July 23, 2000, Section 3, p. 1; Prepared Testimony Of J. Craig Venter, Ph.D., President, and Chief Scientific Officer Celera Genomics, APE Corporation, Business

Before The House Committee On Science Subcommittee On Energy And The Environment, *Federal News Service*, April 6, 2000; www.hoovers.com; www.pe-corp.com.
Source for Albert Einstein Healthcare Network information: www.einstein.edu.

Chapter Four

Source for the quote from Robert Frost: Robert Frost, *Mending Wall*, www.bartleby.com.
Source for the managed care statistics: Michael L Figliuolo, Paul D. Mango, and David H. McCormick, "Hospital Heal Thyself," *The McKinsey Quarterly*, 2000 Number 1, pp. 90-97.
Source for the Medicare statistics: "Healthcare Industry Review and Outlook — Third Quarter 1999, Acute Care Hospitals Outlook," *Bank of America*.
Source for the quote from Charles Handy, author of *The Hungry Spirit*: Charles Handy, *The Hungry Spirit*, (Broadway Books, 1999).
Sources for Northwestern Memorial Hospital information include: Bruce Japsen, "New Hospital Deals with Old Problem of Fit with Needs," *Chicago Tribune*, March 25, 1999, p. B1; Deborah Silver, "Radical Procedure," *Building Design & Construction*, June 1, 1999, p. 68; Meera Somasundaram, "Delivery Day for a $580-Mil. Hospital," *Crain's Chicago Business*, March 29, 1999, p. 1; www.nmh.org.
Sources for Walgreen Company information include: Leonard L. Berry; Larry G. Gresham and Kathleen Seiders, "For Love and Money," *Organizational Dynamics*, September 22, 1997, p. 6; Charles R. Walgreens III and L. Daniel Jorndt, "Letter to Shareholders," Walgreen Company 1998 *Annual Report*; www.walgreens.com.
Source for the quote from L. Daniel Jorndt, chairman and chief executive officer, Walgreen Company: James Frederick, "Annual Report Part 1," *Drug Store News*, April 27, 1998, p. 119.
Sources for Rite Aid Corporation information include: James Frederick, "Robotics Rollout Bolsters Rite Aid's Pharmacy Efficiency," *Drug Store News*, August 30, 1999; Al Heller, "Rite Aid's Aggressive Plans Bring About Mixed Results," *Drug Store News*, April 26, 1999, p. 97; Hope Yen, "Rite Aid May Have Right Stuff with New CEO," *Chicago Tribune*, August 20, 2000, p. 7; www.riteaid.com.
Sources for Walgreen Company information include: Leonard L. Berry; Larry G. Gresham and Kathleen Seiders, "For Love and Money," *Organizational Dynamics*, September 22, 1997, p. 6; Kathleen Hickey, "Moving All Over," *Traffic World*, May 3, 1999, p. 48; "Walgreens' Bold Expansion Strategy Keep It On Top," *Chain Drug Review*, April 28, 1997, p. 165; "Walgreens On the March As Jorndt Era Begins," *Chain Drug Review*, April 27, 1998, p. 157; www.walgreens.com.
Source for the quote from *Forbes ASAP*: www.forbes.com.

Chapter Five

Source for the quote from Scott McNealy, cofounder, chairman, and chief executive officer, Sun Microsystems, Inc.: Scott McNealy, "It's Like," *Forbes ASAP*, October 2, 2000.
Sources for Ascension Health information include: Christine Albano, "The Week Ahead," *The Bond Buyer*, October 11, 1999, p. 7; David Barkholz, "Sisters of St. Joe Merger to Create New Company," *Crain's Detroit Business*, October 19, 1998, p. 6; Deanna Bellandi, "Ascension Top Executive Brennan to Retire," *Modern Healthcare*, March 13, 2000, p. 6; Deanna Bellandi, "Shedding Some Layers: Daughters of Charity Closing Regional Headquarters," *Modern Healthcare*, February 9, 1998, p. 8; Deanna Bellandi, "Sizing Up Systems," *Modern Healthcare*, November 1, 1999, p. 38; Judith VandeWater, "Daughters of Charity Unit Reorganizes," *St. Louis Post-Dispatch*, March 17, 1998, p. C7; Andrew Ward, "The Rise of Ascension," *The Bond Buyer*, September 29, 1999, p. 1; Andrew Ward, "Trends in the Region," *The Bond Buyer*, September 17, 1997, p. 28; www.hoovers.com; www.ascensionhealth.org.
Source for the quote from Miguel de Cervantes: www.makingalife.com.
Sources for the Northwestern Memorial Hospital information include: Patricia B. Limbacher, "Investing for the Future," *Modern Healthcare*, March 16, 1998, p. 62; Meera Somasundaram, "Delivery Day for a $580-Mil. Hospital," *Crain's Chicago Business*, March 29, 1999, p. 1.
Source for Dell Computer Corporation information: David Raymond, "Wall Street Demands," *Forbes*, May 31, 1999.

Chapter Six

Source for the quote from Dee W. Hock, founder and chief executive officer emeritus, Visa International, Inc.: M. Mitchell Waldrop, "Dee Hock on Management," *Fast Company*, October 1996, p. 79, www.fastcompany.com.

Source for The Home Depot, Inc. information: Leonard L. Berry; Larry G. Gresham and Kathleen Seiders, "For Love and Money," *Organizational Dynamics*, September 22, 1997, p. 6.

Source for the quote from Charles Handy, author of *The Hungry Spirit*: Charles Handy, *The Hungry Spirit*, (Broadway Books, 1999).

Source for Cerner Corporation information: "A Look At How Software Firms Recruit The Technicians They Need," *Health Data Management*, January, 1999.

Sources for Merck & Company, Inc. information include: Laura Mansnerus, "It Takes a Village to Make an Office," *The New York Times*, November 21, 1999, Section 14NJ, p. 1; David Pilling, "Bone Advance Is All in Week's Work," *Financial Times* (London), November 23, 1999, p. 18; David P. Willis, "Merck and Honeywell Lead Index Higher," *Asbury Park Press*, October 29, 2000, p. B5; www.hoovers.com.

Source for the quote from *Business Week*: I. Jeanne Dugan, Alison Rea and Joseph Weber, "The Best Performers," *Business Week*, March 24, 1997, p. 80.

Sources for the Guidant Corporation information include: David Chung, "Guidant Corp.'s Ron Dollens," *Investor's Business Daily*, March 18, 1999, p. A8; Kim Kelliher, "Fit To Work," *The Press-Enterprise*, June 18, 2000, p. I10; www.hoovers.com; www.guidant.com.

Source for Cerner Corporation information: www.cerner.com.

Sources for medibuy, Inc. information include: Neil Chesanow, "Save Thousands a Year On Medical Supplies," *Medical Economics*, May 8, 2000, p. 55; Gregory Dalton, "Friends. . .For Now," *The Industry Standard*, April 3, 2000; Philip A. Perry, "Shop Talk," *Materials Management in Health Care*, April 2000, pp. 22-24; www.medibuy.com.

Source for the quote from Ron Dollens, president and chief executive officer, Guidant Corporation: David Chung, "Guidant Corp.'s Ron Dollens," *Investor's Business Daily*, March 18, 1999, p. A8.

Source for WebMD Corporation information: Julie Creswell, "What the Heck is Healtheon?" *Fortune*, February 21, 2000, p. 175.

Source for the quote from Jeffrey P. Bezos, founder, chairman, and chief executive officer, Amazon.com, Inc.: Jeffrey P. Bezos, "Letter to Shareholders," Amazon.com, Inc. 1999 *Annual Report*, www.amazon.com.

Chapter Seven

Source for the quote from William W. George, chairman and chief executive officer, Medtronic, Inc.: William W. George, "The Coming Revolution in Health Care," Speech, delivered to the Medtronic Foundation/WebMD-sponsored Patient Summit, Washington, D.C., July 13, 2000.

Sources for the America Online (AOL) information: www.aol.com; www.media.aoltimewarner.com.

Source for the HealthMagic, Inc. information: www.healthcompassnet.com.

Source for China Mobile, Ltd. information: www.cthk.com.

Source for the quote from R. David Yost, chairman and chief executive officer, AmeriSource Health Corporation: Kim Roller, "Totally Dedicated to Distribution," *Drug Store News*, July 17, 2000, p. 13.

Sources for WebMD Corporation information include: Kris Hundley, "Health Care at Internet Speed," *St. Petersburg Times*, September 18, 2000, p. E8; "Healtheon/WebMD to Acquire OnHealth," The Standard, February 16, 2000; www.thestandard.com; www.hoovers.com; www.healtheon.com; www.webmd.com.

Source for the quote from Fred Wiersema: Fred Wiersema, *The New Market Leaders*, (Free Press, 2001).

Sources for United Health Group, Inc. information include: Milt Freudenheim, "United HMO Shifting Power Back To Doctors," *Austin American-Statesman*, November 9, 1999, p. A1; William W. McGuire, M.D., "Letter to Shareholders," United Health Group, Inc. 1999 *Annual Report*; www.unitedhealthgroup.com.

Sources for Amgen, Inc. information include: www.amgen.com; www.hoovers.com.

Source for the quote from Lawrence A. Bossidy, retired chairman, Honeywell, Inc.: Lawrence A.

Bossidy, "Reality-Based Leadership," *Executive Speeches*, August/September 1998, pp. 10-13.
Source for the AmeriSource Health Corporation and Bergen Brunswig Corporation Drug Company information: Al Heller, "Formidable Four Move Ahead Separately, Optimistically," *Drug Store News*, September 21, 1998, p. 11.
Sources for the Cardinal Health, Inc. information: *Ibid*; "The Wall Street Transcript Publishes Analyst Comments on Cardinal Health," *Business Wire*, August 1, 2000.
Sources for McKesson HBOC include: Al Heller, "Formidable Four Move Ahead Separately, Optimistically" *Drug Store News*, September 21, 1998, p. 11; www.riteaid.com.
Source for quote from Philip N. Knight, chief executive officer, president and chairman, Nike Inc.: Tom Peters, "Attack Yourself," *Chicago Tribune*, September 20, 1993, p. 7.
Sources for PSIHealth.net, Inc. information include: www.psihealth.net; www.sickbay.com.

Chapter Eight

Source for the quote from Peter Drucker: James Dale, "The Foremost Business Thinker of Our Age Tells What Is Wrong (And Right) with the New Economy," *Business 2.0*, August 22, 2000, www.business2.com.
Sources for Medtronic, Inc. information: Tim Stevens, "Heart & Soul," *Industry Week*, May 4, 1998, p. 44; www.hoovers.com.
Source for the quote from Jan Carlzon, former chairman and chief executive officer, Scandinavian Airlines System: Jan Carlzon, *Moments of Truth*, (Harper & Row, 1987), p. 32.
Sources for Cerner Corporation information include: Kathleen Doler, "Leaders & Success," *Investor's Business Daily*, September 1, 1992, p. 1; John A. Jones, "Cerner Developing a Unified Hospital Information System," *Investor's Business Daily*, October 28, 1992, p. 34; Neal L. Patterson, "Letter to Our Shareholders, Clients and Associates," Cerner Corporation, 2000 *Annual Report*, www.cerner.com; www.iqhealth.com; www.hoovers.com.
Sources for Johnson & Johnson information include: Bill Griffeth, "Power Lunch – Johnson & Johnson CEO Interview," *CNBC/Dow Jones Business Video*, transcript, January 11, 2000; Ralph S. Larsen, "FrameworkS," *Chief Executive*, May 1, 1999, p. 10; www.jnj.com; www.hoovers.com.
Source for Pfizer, Inc. information: David Stipp, "Why Pfizer Is So Hot," *Fortune*, May 11, 1998, p. 88.
Sources for The Kaiser Foundation Health Plan, Inc. information include: Erick Schonfeld, "Can Computers Cure Health Care?" *Fortune*, March 30, 1998, p. 111; www.hoovers.com; www.kaiser-permanente.org.
Source for LensCrafters, Inc. information: Leonard L. Berry; Larry G. Gresham and Kathleen Seiders, "For Love and Money," *Organizational Dynamics*, September 22, 1997, p. 6.
Sources for The Mayo Clinic information include: Marni Halasa and Ola Fadahunsi, "On the Road to E-Commerce," *The Bond Buyer*, March 2, 2000, p. 10; "Mayo Clinic HealthQuest Launches Online Service for Companies and Their Employees," *Business Wire*, March 16, 1999; www.mayo.edu.
Sources for Millennium Pharmaceuticals, Inc. information include: Jim Papanikolaw, "Deals, Alliances and Technologies Thrust Milliennium Pharma to the Forefront," *Chemical Market Reporter*, November 8, 1999, p. 31; David Stipp, "Hatching a DNA Giant," *Fortune*, May 24, 1999, p. 178; www.mlmn.com.
Source for the quote from Raymond V. Gilmartin, chairman, president and chief executive officer, Merck & Company, Inc.: Raymond V. Gilmartin, Speech, delivered to The Chief Executives' Club of Boston, Boston, MA, January 19, 2000.

Chapter Nine

Source for the quote from Bette Midler: Dr. Mark Albion, "Special Gifts", *Fast Company*, February, 2000, www.fastcompany.com.
Source for Type A and Type B Personality information: Philip G. Zimbardo; Ann L. Weber and Robert Lee Johnson, *Psychology*, Third Edition, (Allyn & Bacon, 2000).
Source for the question of what's important to a plant: Roger Schenke, J. Richard Gaintner, MD, Martin E. Hickey, MD, Robert H. Hodge, Jr., MD, John M. Ludden, MD, Maj. Gen. Leonard M.

Randolph, Jr., MC, "Leading Beyond the Bottom Line," Physician Executive, Vols. 25-27, 2000-01.
Source for the Walgreen Company information: www.walgreens.com.
Sources for Harry Markowitz information include: Bill Barnhart and Bruce Buursma, "Chicagoan Shares Nobel Prize Ideas Guide Investment Decisions Around The World," Chicago Tribune, October 17, 1990, p. 1; Peter L. Bernstein, Against The Gods (John Wiley & Sons, 1996), Chapter 15, for a discussion of the contribution made by Markowitz and an emerging body of knowledge about risk and return; Peter Passell, "Ideas That Changed Wall St. and Fathered Mutual Funds," The New York Times, October 17, 1990, p. D1.

Chapter Ten

Source for the quote from Wayne Gretzky: Paul Dickson, "Official Rules," Washingtonian, April, 1996, p. 44.
Source for Lloyd's of London information: www.lloyds.com.
Source for the quote from Warren E. Buffett, chairman and chief executive officer, Berkshire Hathaway, Inc.: Nikki Tait and Tracy Corrigan, "The Man with the Silver Touch," Financial Times (London), February 7, 1998, p. 7.
Sources for Capital One Financial Corporation information include: Kathleen Day, "Scratching the Surface," The Washington Post, October 30, 2000, p. E1; Charles Fishman, "This is a Marketing Revolution," Fast Company, May 1999, p. 204, www.fastcompany.com; Charles Fishman, "Waiting for Your Call," National Post, May 6, 1999, p. C16.
Source for Harvard Pilgrim Health Care, Inc. information: www.cainbrothers.com.

Chapter Eleven

Source for Forrester Research, Inc. information: Elizabeth W. Boehm, "Sizing Healthcare eCommerce," Forrester Research, Inc., December 1999, p. 13.
Source for the quote from Stephen M. Case, chairman AOL Time Warner, Inc.: Stephen M. Case, Speech, delivered to the CS First Boston Global Telecom Conference, March 9, 2000.
Sources for Massachusetts General Hospital information include: Liz Kowalczyk, "Doctors Go Online with 2D Opinions Pact Will Expand Overseas Program," The Boston Globe, May 10, 2000, p. D1; "Bringing Expert Medical Advice to the World," Mass High Tech, April 17, 2000, p. 2.
Source for the quote from Harvard Business Review: Clayton M. Christensen, Richard Bohmer and John Kenagy, "Will Disruptive Innovations Cure Health Care?" Harvard Business Review, September/October 2000, p. 102.
Sources for Cisco Systems, Inc. information include: Heidi Elliott, "Online System Helps Cisco Balance Supply and Demand," Electronic Business Today, August, 1997, p. 32; John Evan Frook, "Cisco's $1 Billion Web Site," InternetWeek, December 9, 1996; Fauziah Muhtar, "Help for E-Commerce Move," New Straits Times - Computimes (Malaysia), April 13, 2000, p. 4; Chris J. Parker, "Valley's Big 10 and the Winner Is...," The Daily News of Los Angeles, September 20, 1999, p. B1; Scott Thurm, "How to Drive an Express Train At Fast-Moving Cisco," The Sunday Gazette Mail, June 11, 2000, p. 1D; "Cisco Chalks Up $ 64m in Sales a Day," NZ Infotech Weekly (Wellington), February 14, 2000, p. 16; "Strategy Internet Business Mexico," Business Mexico, December 1, 2000; www.hoovers.com; www.cisco.com.
Source for the U.S. Food and Administration (FDA) information: Julie Appleby and Robert Davis, "Porous Safety Net Allows Lethal Medical Mistakes," USA Today, October 11, 2000, p. 1A.
Source for Forrester Research, Inc. information: Elizabeth W. Boehm, "Sizing Healthcare eCommerce," Forrester Research, Inc., December 1999, p. 13; www.forrester.com.
Sources for Kaiser Permanente and MedUnite information include: Milt Freudenheim, "6 Health Plans Are Developing Online Venture," The New York Times, March 30, 2000, p. C1; Christina Le Beau, "Insurance Online," The Industry Standard, April 10, 2000; www.blueshieldca.com.
Sources for Neoforma.com, Inc. and e-MedSoft.com information include: Lynne Brakeman, "Experts Say That MCOs Leave Billions on the Table," Managed Healthcare, April, 2000, p. 50; Ted Hartzell, "E-Shopping for Medical Supplies," www.knowledgespace.com, Arthur Andersen, January 17, 2000; Barbara Murphy, "e-MedSoft to Acquire Illumea for Common Stock," Los Angeles Times,

May 2, 2000, p. B6; "e-MedSoft.com Healthcare Meets Genetics," Arthur Andersen, Player Profiles, www.knowledgespace.com.
Sources for University Medical Associates and MacGregor Medical Association information include: Donald Berwick, M.D., "Knowledge Always On Call," *Modern Healthcare*, September 27, 1999, p. S2; Alice Dragoon, "A Cure for Broken Records," CIO, February 1, 1997; Arthur Andersen, knowledge-space.com interviews with Dr. James Birge, CEO and Medical Director; Larry White, CIO; and Laura Cook, RN and CQO; "Infinium Software's e-Business Solutions Win 'Powered By AS/400e' Award From IBM," *Business Wire*, March 30, 1999; www.infinium.com; www.macgregor.com.

Chapter Twelve

Source for the quote from John F. Welch Jr., chairman and chief executive, General Electric Company: John F. Welch, "Speed, Simplicity, Self-Confidence," *Harvard Business Review*, September-October 1989, p. 112.
Source for the Securities and Exchange Commission (SEC) information: Amy Higgins, "Every One An Insider," *The Cincinnati Enquirer*, October 21, 2000, p.C1.
Sources for the Applera Corporation information include: Julie Bell, "Man Behind Genome Map Leader," *The Baltimore Sun*, July 30, 2000, p. 1D; Andrew Pollack, "The Microsoft (and Gates) of the Genome Industry," *The New York Times*, July 23, 2000, Section 3, p. 1; www.hoovers.com.
Source for the Pl-x.com information: www.pl-x.com.
Source for the Intellectual Property Technology Exchange, Inc. information: www.techex.com.
Source for the patentauction.com information: www.patentauction.com.
Source for the BTG plc information: www.btgplc.com.
Sources for the Chemdex information include: www.chemdex.com; www.hoovers.com.
Sources for Medscape, HealthGrades.com, and Medline information include: Jeremy Kahn, "HealthGrades: Playing Doctor On the Web," *Fortune*, December 6, 1999, p. 318; Laura Landro, "Just The Facts," *Pittsburgh Post-Gazette*, July 25, 2000, p. C2; Player Profiles, Arthur Andersen, www.knowledgespace.com; www.nlm.nih.gov.
Source for Cyber Dialogue information: Christian Le Beau, "Insurance Online," *Industry Standard*, April 3, 2000.
Source for the Cisco Systems, Inc. information: Beth Belton and Del Jones, "Cisco Chief," *USA Today*, October 12, 1999, p. 3B.

Chapter Thirteen

Source for the Hippocrates and the Hippocratic Oath information: "The Doctor's World," *The New York Times*, May 15, 1990, p. C3.
Source for the *Journal of the American Medical Association* information: "For Our Patients, Not for Profits," *Journal of the American Medical Association*, December 3, 1997.
Source for Gerald Greens's best-seller, *The Last Angry Man*, information: Gerald Green, *The Last Angry Man* (Amereon Ltd. 1983).
Source for the Celera Genomics Group information: www.celera.com.

INDEX

A

Abrashoff, D. Michael, Captain, 39
Accounts payable, 25
Accounts receivable, 84, 173
Aetna U.S. Healthcare, 99, 192
Albert Einstein Healthcare, 42-43
   allhealth.com, 99
AOL Time Warner, 99-102, 112
AmeriSource Health, 108-110, 193
Amgen, 77-78, 105-107, 152
Applera, 40-41, 203-204
Applied Biosystems, 40, 203-204
Ascension Health, 72-74
Avnet, 186

B

Business-to-business (B2B), 189, 193, 195
Baker, Charles D., 172
Balance sheet, 10-11, 16, 25-26, 32, 34, 41,
   43-46, 57, 62, 70, 79, 86, 202
Banner Health, 92
Baptist/St. Vincent's Health, 73
Baxter International, 39
Bergen Brunswig, 108-110
Berwick, Donald, M.D., 195
Bezos, Jeffrey P., 94
Biotechnology, 13, 18, 27, 78, 105-106, 134,
   216, 222
Blue Shield of California, 192
Book and market value, 9-11, 25-26, 57, 112,
   147, 150, 157, 202-205, 209
Bossidy, Lawrence A., 107
Boudreau, Donald L., 128

Browne, David, 130
BTG plc, 206
Buckley, William F., Jr., 129
Buffett, Warren E., 167
Business risk, 165, 175, 184
   Business risk management process, 174
Business risk model, 166
Byron, Lord, 74

C

Cancer, 13-14, 106, 117, 126
Capital One, 167-172
Cardinal Health, 108-109
Carlzon, Jan, 121
Case, Stephen M., 183
Celera Genomics Group, 40, 203-204, 225
Cerner, 85, 90, 121-123
Cervantes, Miguel de, 73
Chambers, John T., 29
Champy, James, 126
China Mobile, 100
Cigna, 192
Cisco Systems, 185-188, 210
Clark, James, 93-94
Cleveland Clinic, 184
ClinicalTrials.gov, 208
Cook, Rick, 104-105
Crick, Francis, 7-8
Customer Assets, 33, 46, 100-104, 106,
   111-112, 136, 147, 150, 168, 192, 205, 208
   Affiliates, 46, 107, 110-112
   Channels, 34, 46, 98, 100, 107-108, 111-112,
   147, 205

Customers, 11-12, 14-18, 28, 33-35, 46, 62,
   66, 74, 86, 90-91, 93-95, 100-112, 122-123,
   126, 130-131, 134, 140, 148-149, 153, 155-
   158, 167-171, 177, 183, 185-191, 197, 204-
   205,
   207-208, 210, 220, 223
CVS, 94
Cyber Dialogue, 208, 219-220

D

Damark International, 170-171
Darwin, Charles, 8
Daughters of Charity National Health System
   (DCNHS), 72-74
Dell Computer, 77
Dell, Michael S., 40
Dickens, Charles, 12
Digital markets, 13
Discounted cash flow, 112
Disney, Walt, 85
DNA, 2, 8, 10, 13, 40, 203-204
Dollens, Ron, 91
Drucker, Peter, 117
Duke University Health, 184
DYG, 27

E

E-commerce, 13, 17, 34-35, 66, 136, 191
e-Medsoft.com, 193-194
Ebusiness, 190
Economic DNA, 3, 10, 13, 19
Edwards, Brooks, Dr., 133
Eli Lilly, 87, 94
Employee and supplier assets, 45, 79, 92, 95
Employees, 11, 15-18, 25, 27-29, 33-35, 43, 45,
   65-66, 83-89, 93, 95, 110, 117-120, 122, 124,
   129, 131-132, 134, 140, 149, 152, 155-158,
   167, 170-171, 177, 186, 190-191, 194, 207,
   210, 223
Partners, 45-46, 66, 73-74, 84, 92-93, 95, 147,
   156, 177, 186, 192, 197
Suppliers, 11, 15-16, 29, 33-35, 43, 56, 66,
   83-84, 89-92, 95, 109, 112, 131, 140, 149,
   155-157, 166-167, 185-186, 190, 192-193,
   197, 204, 210, 220, 223

F

Fairbank, Richard D., 167-169
Federal Reserve, 31
Financial assets, 17, 26, 34, 45, 66, 69-72, 74,
   78-79, 84, 140, 147, 165, 167
   Cash, 27, 34, 45, 71-72, 74, 76-77, 79, 84,
   147, 155, 209
   Debt, 25, 34, 45, 72-74, 76, 79, 147,
   170, 205
   Equity, 34, 45, 74-75, 77, 79, 109, 147, 205
   Investment, 9, 17, 26-28, 31, 35, 43-45, 47,
   58, 61, 72, 74-76, 79, 84, 127, 140, 146-
   147, 149-153, 155-157, 174, 188, 209, 217
   Receivables, 45, 74, 79, 84
Fisher Scientific International, 193
Food and Drug Administration (FDA), 109,
   188-189
Forrester Research, 182, 189-190
Foundation Health, 192
Friedman, Meyer, 145-146
Frost, Robert, 55

G

Gartner Group, 188
Genome, 9, 11, 51
   Business genome, 3, 9-10, 19, 40-41, 43-
   44, 47, 148
   Human genome, 2, 8-9, 13, 25, 40, 134,
   204, 224
George, William W., 26-27, 99, 117-121
Gilmartin, Raymond V., 17, 135
Goldsmith, Martin, 42
Green, Gerald, 217
Greenspan, Alan, 31
Gretzky, Wayne, 163
Guidant, 87-89

H

Hammer, Michael, 126
Handy, Charles, 16, 57, 84
Hartford Company The, 170
Harvard Pilgrim Health Care, 167, 172-173
Hawken, Paul, 28-29
Health Oasis, 132-133
HealthCompass, 99

HealthGrades.com, 208
HealthMagic, 99
HealthQuest, 132-133
Hippocrates, 215-216
Hippocratic Oath, 215-218, 225
Hock, Dee W., 83
Home Depot, 84-85
Humana, 94

I

IBM, 194
Income statements, 25, 43
Infinium Software, 194
Inova Health, 91
Inventory, 25, 35, 44, 58, 64-66, 84, 91, 110, 136, 149, 186, 209
Intangible assets, 3, 10-11, 16-19, 26-28, 33-35, 41, 43, 56-57, 66, 84, 101, 111, 118, 121, 150, 155-158, 165, 167, 172, 177, 196, 204, 207, 209
Intel, 77-78, 189
Intelihealth.com, 99
Intellectual capital, 11, 27, 155, 157-158
Intellectual property, 111, 134, 136, 157, 205-206, 217, 219
Intellectual Property Technology Exchange, 205
IQHealth, 122-123

J

Jabil Circuit, 186
James, Mike, 120
Johns Hopkins, 184
Johnson & Johnson, 124-125, 153
Jorndt, L. Daniel, 63

K

Kaiser, Henry J., 118, 127-128
Kaiser Foundation, 127-129
Kaiser Permanete, 128, 192
Knight, Philip N., 110
Kraus, Irene, Sister, 72

L

Larsen, Ralph J., 125
LensCrafters, 130-131
Levin, Arthur, 32
Liabilities, 24-25
Lloyds of London, 165
Luxottica, 130

M

MacGregor Medical Association, 194-195
Majeske, Mark, 108
Malone, Bruce, Dr., 104
Malone, Michael S., 26
Marcus, Bernie, 84
Markowitz, Harry, 151-152
Marsh, Lawrence C., 109
Massachusetts General Hospital, 183
Mathews, Katherine, 88
Mayo, Charles, 132
Mayo, William, 132
Mayo Clinic, 132-134
McGuire, William W., M.D., 105
MCI WorldCom, 101, 171
McKesson HBOC, 108, 110, 193
McNealy, Scott, 71, 190
Mecklenburg, Gary, 58-61
medibuy.com, 90-92
Medline, 129, 208
Medscape, 208
Medtronic, 26-27, 90, 117-119, 121, 153
MedUnite, 192
Mendel, Gregor, 7-8
Merck, 17, 85-87, 135
Microsoft, 31, 77
Midler, Bette, 145
Millennium Pharmaceuticals, 134-135
Morris, Nigel W., 167-168

N

Neoforma.com, 193
Netscape, 93
Net worth, 24-25, 172
Neu, David, 108, 110
New Economy, 24

Nike, 110
Northwestern Memorial, 58-61, 75-76

O

Onhealth.com, 102
Organization assets, 44, 46, 63, 78-79, 107,
    111, 118, 126, 136, 147, 167, 173
    Brand, 44, 46, 56, 111, 118, 131-134, 155,
    157, 172, 204, 209
    Culture and values, 44, 46, 118, 129
    Innovation, 46, 167-169, 171, 224
    Intellectual property, 78, 134, 136, 157,
    205, 217, 219
    Knowledge, 17, 29, 46, 130, 177, 209
    Leadership, 44, 46, 111, 118, 147
    Process, 10, 46, 126, 168, 170-171, 173-
    177, 185, 190-193, 195-197, 224
    Strategy, 46, 121-123, 126-127, 175
    Structure, 46, 118, 123-124, 126, 157, 174
    Systems, 44, 46, 56, 111, 118, 127, 156,
    173-175, 191, 195-197
Owens & Minor, 193

P

PacifiCare Health, 192
Panoply, 127, 205
Partners HealthCare, 184
Pasteur, Louis, 204
The Patent & License Exchange, 205
Patentauction.com, 206
PathNet, 122
Patterson, Neal L., 123
Perkin-Elmer, 39-40, 203
Pfizer, 126-127
Physical assets, 17, 25, 43-45, 47, 54, 56-59,
    61-62, 66, 84, 101, 147, 150, 155, 176
    Buildings, 27, 32, 41, 44, 56, 58, 61-62, 64,
    66, 155
    Equipment, 10, 14, 27, 39, 44, 56-57, 59,
    62-65, 84, 90-91, 110, 119, 127-128, 130,
    152, 166, 186, 193, 203, 216, 220
    Inventory, 25, 44, 58, 64-66, 84, 91, 110,
    136, 149, 186
    Land, 44, 56, 58, 61-62, 66, 84, 155

Pl-x.com, 205
Principi, Eugene, 76
Proprietary knowledge, 25-26, 46, 107,
    134-135, 185, 223
PSIHealth.net, 111

R

Rapid Script, 63-64
Real estate, 25, 62
Reich, Robert, 25
Ridley, Matt, 8
Rite Aid, 63, 110
Rosenman, Ray, 145-146
Rubric, 118

S

ScriptPro USA, 63-64
Securities and Exchange Commission
    (SEC), 201
Sickbay.com, 111
Signet, 168
Silicon Graphics, 93
Sisters of St. Joseph Health, 72-73
Solvik, Peter, 186-187
Smith, Hedrick, 31
Strategic Inventory Management System
    (SIMS), 64
Sun Microsystems, 71, 190
Sword, Stanley, 84-85

T

Tangible assets, 10-11, 16, 23, 25, 34, 79, 84,
    146, 155, 157, 165, 196
TechEx, 205
Toyota, 90
Type A and type B personality, 146

U

U.S. Bancorp Piper Jaffray, 193
U.S. Institute for Medicine, 32
UnitedHealth Group, 103-105
University Medical Associates (UMA), 194

V

Value creation, 9, 15, 19, 41, 118, 147, 150, 155, 194, 210, 216-218, 220, 225

Value Dynamics Framework, 10, 33, 44-45, 47, 107, 118, 124, 127, 148, 155

Venter, J. Craig, 40

W

Wagner, Gary, 91

Walgreen, 61-66, 150-151

Wal-Mart, 61

Watson, James, 8

WebMD, 93-94, 102-103, 189

Welch, John F., Jr., 201

WellPoint Health Systems, 192

Wells, H. G., 164

Western Maryland Health, 73

Weston, Gary, 92

White, Tony L., 39-40, 203-204

Widman, Jerry, 73

Wiersema, Fred, 103

Wolf, Ron, 18

WorldCare, 183-184, 189

Y

Yost, David R., 100, 108-109

Young, Arthur, 58

Z

Zeitgeist, 33